100% OFFICIAL

WHERE WE ARE

OUR BAND OUR STORY

HARPER

An Imprint of HarperCollinsPublishers

WHERE·WE·ARE

OUR BAND
OUR STORY

Hi everyone,

We're very excited to welcome you to *Where We Are*. We hope you enjoy reading it as much as we enjoyed writing it!

When we look back over our time in 1D so far, we can hardly believe everything that's happened to us. There are so many things we're proud of, but the ones that really stand out are having three number-one albums (and particularly all of the writing we have done on *Midnight Memories*), all of our tours (which have been incredible), winning some amazing awards and our first-ever movie, *This Is Us*, becoming a number-one box office hit.

We owe it all to you, the fans. If we tried to express how grateful we are to each and every one of you, we'd run out of words, so we'll keep it simple - THANK YOU x

Lots of love,

Louis, Liam, Harry, Niall and Zayn
May 2014

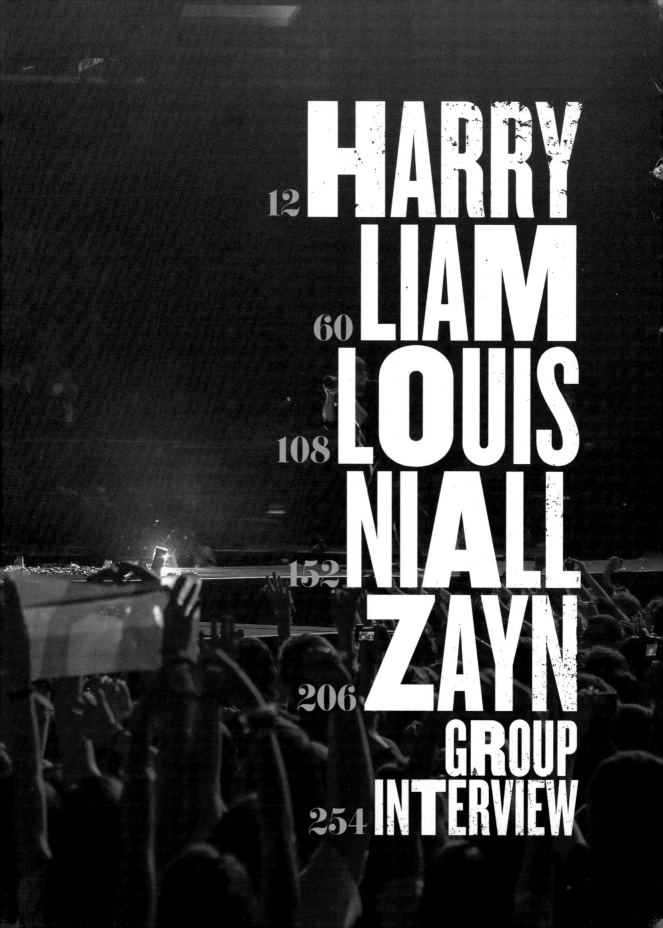

LAUNCH

WHERE
WE'VE
COME
FROM

It's impossible to put into words how much my life has changed since *The X Factor*. For a start I live in London now, I'm in a band and I get to travel to amazing places... It's ridiculous when I think about it!

When I compare us now to us in the early days of *The X Factor*, I know we've improved so much as a group. In everything from harmonies and movement to understanding what it is to be onstage and be in a group. I think we've gained a lot of confidence and we all feel that we can really be ourselves in front of the crowd.

As much as my life is totally different to how it used to be, in some ways things haven't changed that much, because I can still live a normal life. People always ask me, "Is it impossible to do all the things you used to do?" but actually I can still go for a drink or dinner and not be bothered. I just have to be a bit cleverer about it than I used to be.

If I just want to go out somewhere I try not to think about it too much. I just go and do it. You could drive yourself crazy worrying about whether it's safe, and you have to live your life. I know that there are certain places where people know me, or their friends do, and if they recognize me they won't be bothered.

There are times when things can get a bit intrusive, but you just have to get on with it. If you're walking down the street and someone takes a picture, so what? You're in public, so you kind of expect it, and it's not a big deal. But if someone were to take photos of me in my house, that would bother me. You have to have somewhere that's private.

One of the mottos that I've learned since I joined the band that I try to stick by is: "Work hard, play hard and be kind" – because it works. In order to have a good time you have to work hard to be successful, and being kind to people should be a given. If everyone was a little bit nicer to people, the world would be a much better place. You have a choice where you can either be all right to someone or you can be a little bit nicer, and that can make someone's day.

Harry

ABOVE: Kicking off the *Take Me Home* world tour at the O2 Arena in London. 23 February 2013

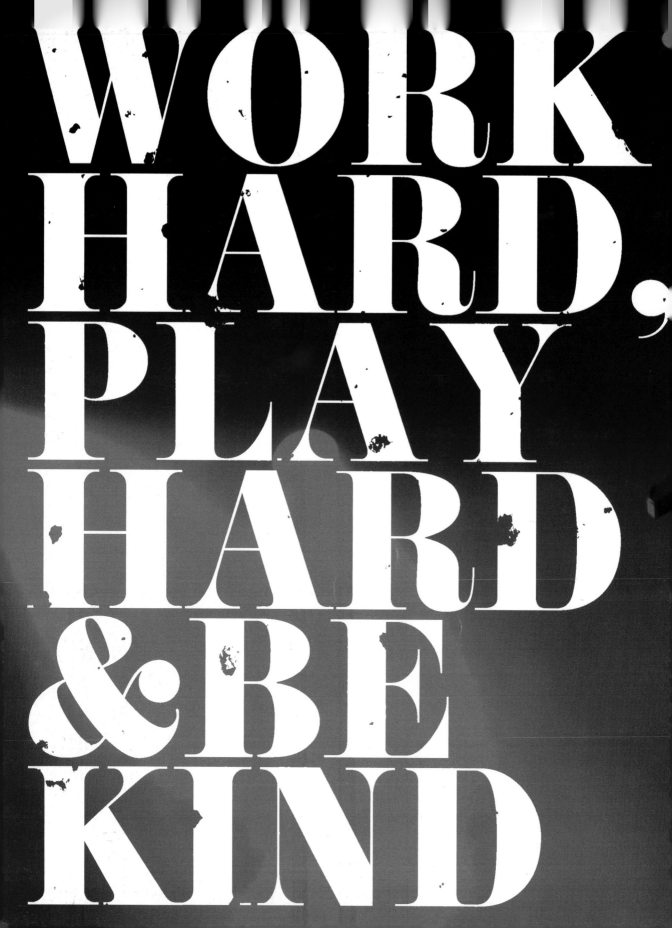

TAKE OFF

WHERE WE'VE BEEN

W e've been so lucky because we've been able to go to some incredible places. Of the places we've visited so far Sydney is one of my favorites. It's pretty English – it's a lot like London in terms of their culture and the way people are – but everything's just a bit happier because the weather is great, and things move slightly more slowly because people are chilled out.

I also love LA, although I think you have to make it your own. If you go there not knowing anyone it's not that great, because you need to know where to go and how to get there. If you have friends you can meet at parties and restaurants, LA is the best place in the world. But if you were on your own you'd feel quite lonely.

New York is very different to LA but equally brilliant. In New York you can go out and meet people really easily. There's stuff going on every night and it's always so busy that you could easily go out in the early evening and stay out until morning. It's like London there too, but sped up. If you were staying in New York and you woke up with jet lag at 4am and wanted to see a gig, there would probably be one going on somewhere. No one really eats until 10pm and dinner will go on until 1am. It's very cool. You can people-watch in New York too, which I really enjoy.

We've met some incredible people on our travels. Michelle Obama was great, and I think she and Barack probably really are just the way they come across in the press – very normal. They're being themselves, they just happen to have ridiculously high-profile jobs. I think Michelle is an amazing First Lady. Everyone seems to love her, and I think that's because she's so warm and kind.

Happy red nose day!
15 March 2013

Personally, when we've been traveling I've always tried to meet locals and see how they are in their hometown. When we were in Chicago someone from our record label introduced me to a couple of local guys. I played golf with them and it was nice to go out and do something different. Coincidentally, they used to be mates with Barack Obama and play golf with him every Sunday, and they said he's really down to earth. One of the guys even invited me over to his house for a barbecue, so I went over and met his family. Things like that are really special.

Going to Ghana for Comic Relief was an unbelievable, life-changing experience. I was so humbled by all of the people we met, and really moved by what we saw. The fact that Comic Relief raised such an incredible amount of money means so much to us, because it will make a huge difference to so many lives. If I was asked to go again, I would in a second.

I haven't learned any languages yet, but I really want to learn sign language. So many people can speak different languages, but if you could make a difference to that one person who can't communicate it would be amazing. I met a girl and her mom in Ireland once and they both signed, and I signed "thank you" back to them and they couldn't believe it.

If someone who was using sign language came to your show or your book signing and you could sign back to them, it would be such a good feeling. I think that's much nicer than being able to order steak and chips in French. So the plan is to learn much more sign language as soon as I get a chance.

I'm not a big shopper when we're traveling, so amazingly I save money when I'm away. Especially when we're touring. I'll pick things up here and there, but I can't get that much in my suitcase! Also, I can't do online shopping because I've got nowhere for it to be delivered to when we're moving around so much. I tend to pick up little trinkets to remember places by, or gifts for people.

I've never told anyone this before but I did pick up an interesting souvenir in LA once. We were invited to meet Johnny Depp's daughter, so we went over to his studio. My friend was texting me saying, "You have to rob something and bring it back." So I've got this little pink bar of soap from Johnny Depp's toilet that I nicked. He's going to think I'm a freak if he reads this!

We've been on so many TV shows around the world now, but one we did in Japan really stands out because it was the most ridiculous thing ever. There was confetti all over the place and there were tons of crew and it was so fast paced. It was so crazy we didn't really know what was going on.

ONE DIRECTION ISN'T JUST ABOUT THE BAND, IT'S ABOUT ALL THE PEOPLE WHO HAVE HELPED US ALONG THE WAY

In terms of live shows, playing Madison Square Garden for the first time was a real "moment" for us. The nice thing was that pretty much everyone who's worked on One Direction as a project was there, from the guy who designed our first album cover to song producers.

One Direction isn't just about the band, it's about all the people who have helped us along the

Where WE ARE

Even though a lot of crazy things are going on around us, I honestly don't think it's been that hard to stay down to earth. I look around me and I can see how people could get carried away, because if you lived completely in the fame bubble you could end up thinking you're the greatest thing ever. I almost feel a bit sorry for people whose lives get completely taken over by it, because I can see how it would be hard to stay grounded. But we all live very normal lives outside of the band, so we don't let things run away with us.

My family is amazing. They treat me exactly the same way as they always did – and there's no reason why they shouldn't. My friends from home are the same. I think you just need to take a step back from it every now and again, remind yourself of what it is you're involved in as a whole and get it in perspective. It's a very cool job, but it doesn't make me any better than anybody else.

I'm very aware of little things, like saying that people work "with" us rather than "for" us. I hate hearing people say that others work for them – I'm sure they only do it because it makes them feel important. We're all working hard for the same goal.

ABOVE: On a shoot for *AERA* magazine.
18 January 2013

One of my friends jokes around with me if I walk through a door before her. She'll say, "Do you do that because you're famous? Hold the door open for me!" I love it when people rib me about things.

If you're not very nice to people, word gets around. When someone meets you for the first time, there's no gray area. They'll go back to their friends and either say "he was really nice" or "he's a bit of an idiot to be honest," because saying someone is "all right" isn't a great story.

If you act even slightly like a diva, people will pick up on it. If I see someone acting like they're something special it shocks me into not doing it even more. And I have seen a lot of people do it, both famous and non-famous. I don't understand why you can't just be nice to people, whether you're in the public eye or not.

SOME PEOPLE ONLY HAVE "**YES**" PEOPLE AROUND THEM, WHO TELL THEM THEY'RE WONDERFUL ALL OF THE TIME **&** THEY CAN **LOSE** PERSPECTIVE

I surround myself with people who do all kinds of jobs, and I like going out to all sorts of places that aren't to do with the industry. Also, my friends will tell me if I'm doing something wrong or if something I'm wearing looks ridiculous, and not everyone has that. Some people only have "yes" people around them, who tell them they're wonderful all of the time, and they can lose perspective.

I think it's nice to give back, and I don't think there's anything wrong with buying my mom a present if I want to, but I try to buy people things that they need rather than random big gifts. You can end up looking like a massive show-off if you turn up with loads of gifts for Christmas or someone's birthday, because it looks like you're trying to trump everyone else's presents. Plus, if you give things to people all of the time they stop meaning anything. I prefer giving thoughtful presents. Anyone can buy something expensive if they have the money, but it's harder to buy something that means something to someone.

MUSIC & MORE

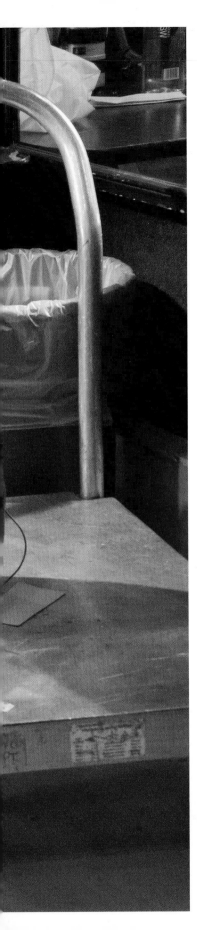

It still hasn't sunk in that we went to number one in so many countries with both of our albums. When we go and visit all those countries – which we are planning to do – it will sink in much more.

We found out we were number one in Australia while we were over there doing promo, so we could kind of get it, but when you just see a lot of figures written down on a sheet of paper it doesn't seem real. It's tough to picture it. I try to process it when I'm lying in bed at night. I'll stop and think, "I cannot believe we went to number one in the Philippines."

Some people say that One Direction is half our look and half our music. I don't think we've ever relied just on our look; our music has to be strong for us to stay in the position we are. The main reason the music has to be great is because of the fans. We are a musical group and we love what we do. We couldn't sing songs we don't believe in.

We're quite vulnerable to critics, because we were put together on a reality show. I get that some people don't like that, and that's fine. Everyone is entitled to their likes and dislikes. However, if our music did drop off, it would only be right for people to have a bit of a go at us, because at the end of the day we're a band.

If our music wasn't good, people would think all we do is mess around and look all right. But you need good music to back all of that up. We feel like our music is getting stronger all the time. Some people may not like us, but we do make a really good pop song, and they'd still dance to it at a wedding.

WE ARE A MUSICAL GROUP & WE LOVE WHAT WE DO. WE COULDN'T SING SONGS WE DON'T BELIEVE IN

Of course it's amazing to get recognition for our music, so winning awards means so much to us. My favorite awards ceremony to date has been the VMAs. I didn't even expect us to be invited, because it's such a big deal. So for us to be invited, then asked to perform and then to win three awards was unbelievable.

The BRITs is always a great night as well. We were so excited to go to our first one in 2012, and when we won the award for British Single we were stunned. Then we performed in 2013 and we absolutely loved it. It was great getting to sing "One Way or Another (Teenage Kicks)," because Comic Relief is such an important charity.

At the moment my house is being renovated and I'm staying between two friends' houses, so the awards we've been given are all over the place. Two are on a friend's windowsill, some others are in my other friend's bedroom and one of my other mates has got another one. One of the EMAs has been swiped by my friend's sister, so I need to try to get that back. The others are in storage, and I'll be getting them out when I move back home.

FABULOUS FANS

I can still remember the feeling we used to get when we went into the *X Factor* studios right back at the beginning. When there were fans outside we used to be so excited, and I still get the same feeling now.

When there are a lot of people outside a venue it shocks me. Sometimes I think people won't turn up to a TV studio if it's in the middle of nowhere, but they do and it's so nice.

When we did the *Today* show in New York we didn't know what the reaction would be like. It was our first proper show in America and we were nervous. We knew from Twitter and Facebook that we had a bit of a fanbase there, but an amazing number of fans turned up to welcome us, and to see things on that scale was ridiculous. There were so many people there.

A lot of people try to make it in America, and I think we've been incredibly lucky timing-wise, because there hasn't been a boy band out there for a while. I think it's a great time for British music in America at the moment generally, with the likes of Adele and Ed Sheeran; they're doing unbelievably well. And it's down to the fans spreading the word about UK music.

We've known some of the fans for three years, and they still come and make the effort to see us. For us, that's been one of the nicest parts of the whole thing, because we know their names and we can ask them about their lives. It's great seeing some of the old faces – and also lots of new faces.

The fans have been incredible to us. They don't vary much around the world – they're universally amazing. Sometimes there's no time to do much more than have a picture taken with them if things are hectic, but it's nice when there aren't many fans in one place, because then you get a chance to sit down and chat to them. I was talking to some fans the other night who are at uni, and it's crazy to think that if I weren't in the band I would probably be in the same position as them. Or even at uni with them.

THE FANS
HAVE BEEN
INCREDIBLE
TO US. THEY
DON'T VARY
MUCH AROUND
THE WORLD —
THEY'RE
UNIVERSALLY
AMAZING

We love performing and seeing the fans, so touring is probably my favorite thing to do. When it comes to traveling, I think what we all enjoy most is being on the tour bus. You can chill out, have some food and go to sleep when you want to. I try not to do too much. I'll watch a film and chat to the boys, but it's nice to have proper downtime to catch up with friends and family.

We do have a really good laugh if we're in a stupid mood. I remember once we decided to jokingly attack Paul, our tour manager. I was naked and I thought it would be a really quick fight, but it took forever, so I was stuck in a naked headlock for about ten minutes...

The crew is like one big tour family, and I think if you didn't have that community feel you would go crazy. You're away from your family and friends, so you need that support network of people who are there for you. I can always talk to the boys, but I know I can talk to the crew too. Everyone needs everyone, and we're all on each other's side.

Even though you're away from home and you're working long hours when you're touring, you do get a chance to recharge your batteries a bit. You can have a lie-in and you can get into a good routine. You know that you can go to the gym, have some lunch and then head to the venue at a set time.

The beds on the tour bus are pretty comfortable, and the American buses are always massive, so you get bigger beds and DVD players in the bunks. I always take a scented candle with me when I travel because it reminds me of home, and I also light them in the dressing room before a gig sometimes. It's nice to have a touch of home.

I think the thing that people like about our shows is that you get something different all the time. We always mess around onstage and there are always little jokes going on, which I think is nice for the crowd.

The last night of the tour is the one that I'd want to go and see, because pretty much everything falls apart. The crew come on and throw things at us when we're performing, and you can do everything you've always wanted to do onstage because it's the last one. It's the fun show, and I think if you came and saw it you'd have a laugh. It's always a longer show too, because we're doing so much stupid stuff. I'd love to watch one back. It's probably awful, but great fun!

The world tour is huge for us, so we took our time making sure every single detail of it was right. We came up with ideas for the lighting, the screens and all the things that previously we hadn't had time to get so involved in. It's our show at the end of the day, so we want it to reflect who we are. Our ultimate goal was to make a show that we would enjoy watching ourselves.

The tour is going to many different countries and we want everyone to come and have an incredible time with us. We feel so proud of it. I'm loving every second of it. If I could go back and start it all again tomorrow, I would.

WHERE NEXT?

Where WE'RE GOING

We were both nervous and excited about making the 1D movie. There's so much that we do that people don't see, so it's nice to let fans get an insight into who we really are. We put everything out there – nothing was hidden.

We do mess around a lot, so it was great fun making it, and you definitely get to see the ridiculous side of us. Well, the even more ridiculous side.

It was a really natural process and nothing was set up – a lot of the time we forgot the cameras were there. It wasn't like we decided to go water-skiing or anything just to make the film more interesting. If the cameras missed something, the producers didn't ask us to set it up again so they could film it, because that wouldn't have worked. We were just us.

While we've been on the road we've also been working on the third album, and it's been really exciting because we're writing a lot more. We're experimenting more with this album, which has been great. We want to make the third album our best yet.

We by no means feel like we're at the top of our game. We always want to push further and be the best we can be. There's still so much more we can do. I'm excited to see what happens. I want to carry on working hard, playing hard and being kind!

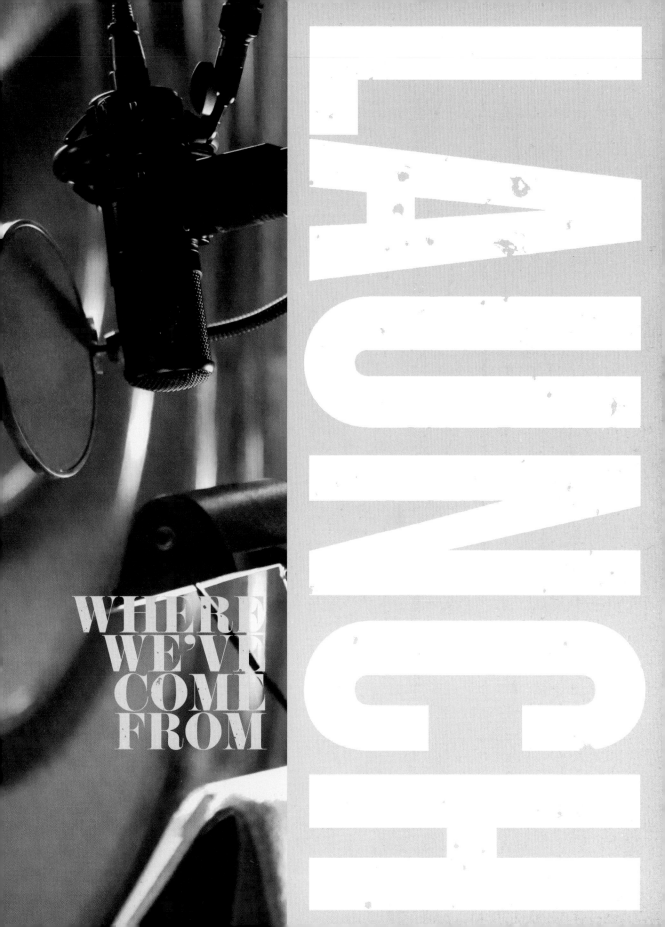

LAUNCH

WHERE
WE'VE
COME
FROM

Liam and the Barlow!
22 August 2012

Liam

Our lives have changed so much since we all auditioned for *The X Factor*. I guess the biggest change is how busy we are. I can't believe I'm in a job where we work such silly hours, especially when I look back at how lazy I used to be!

We do work crazy hours sometimes, but we just get on with it and don't think about it, because we're so grateful to be in this position. It's so rewarding and we really enjoy our work. I do get tired from time to time, and sometimes when I wake up in the morning I can think of nothing nicer than staying in bed all day... But once I'm showered and dressed and with the boys I'm raring to go.

I'm totally used to having jet lag now, and sometimes I even quite enjoy it. If my body clock is a bit off and I wake up in the night, I love the feeling of looking at my watch and knowing that I've got loads more time left to sleep.

Twitter time in Dublin.
6 March 2012

THIS IS EVERYTHING I'VE EVER WANTED TO DO

Day 2 of the Take Me Home tour.
Liam is in the zone...
24 February 2013

THIS IS BRILLIANT FUN, I'M HAVING SUCH A LAUGH WITH MY MATES

Having four other crazy lads around is the best way to stay upbeat when you're tired. We don't take anything too seriously and we don't let anything go to our heads. I never think, "Look at us, we're on another TV show," I just think, "This is brilliant fun, I'm having such a laugh with my mates."

It's so hard to sit down and try to choose my favorite 1D moments to date, because there have been a ridiculous number of them. If I had to pinpoint some I would say the EMAs, playing at Madison Square Garden and being on the tour bus with the other lads, any time at all, really.

Being onstage at Madison Square Garden was amazing. We got to have a B-stage and pop up out of the floor and all sorts of stuff. It was so much fun and it's such a prestigious place, so looking out and knowing that everyone was there for us was quite something.

I also love it when we get a couple of weeks off, because it gives us a chance to sit back, look at the craziness of everything that's happened and really reflect on it.

It's very strange to look back to the early days and see how far we've come.

IT'S A WHOLE NEW WORLD

I still find it incredible when I think about all of the places we've been able to visit so far. Australia is one of my favorite places in the world. I loved it and I loved learning to surf with Louis. We also went out on a boat and sailed all around Sydney Harbor and saw the Opera House.

Japan is great too, and I've got top memories of San Diego because I caught a tiger shark by accident! We'd been fishing all day and I'd only caught really small fish, so I decided I was a bit rubbish at it. Then I left my rod in for ages and suddenly I saw a tug... When I pulled my line in there was a three-foot baby tiger shark hanging off of it! It was only the second time I'd been fishing and by the end I felt like a pro.

I love trying new things in the different places we visit. Louis has always been very outgoing, but I wasn't like that at all. Now he convinces me to experiment and it's made me more confident. It's brilliant, because it means that I get to learn more about the cultures of the places we go to.

Bungee jumping was invented in New Zealand, so when we were there we really wanted to do it, but we couldn't for insurance reasons. We found something else called a Sky Fall that was considered safer, so we gave that a go instead. It was still scary, though, and not great for anyone who doesn't like heights as you literally fly through the air. I like stepping outside of my comfort zone and trying new foods and activities. It's a whole new world.

Going to Africa for Comic Relief was absolutely one of the best things I've ever done. It was a life-changing trip. There hasn't been one day since we've been that I haven't thought about it; it's often the last thing I think about before I go to sleep at night.

I've watched videos that people have done for Comic Relief over the years, but they're nothing compared to how you feel when you're actually there. It's very sad and moving, but it's also so inspiring to see how incredible the people are in poverty-stricken places. We went to the slums in Ghana and, even though they've got nothing, the people are so happy there. If you walk down the street in London everyone seems miserable and they're always busy looking at their mobile phones, but over there people wave and smile and come and say hello.

It's very strange to look back to the early days and see how far we've come. It's weird because it feels like we've been in the band for ages, but at the same time it's gone so quickly. I'm excited about what else is to come.

We visited a children's hospital and that was really heartbreaking. I wanted to try to help out, but I had no idea what I could do to make things better for them. It made me wish I had some kind of medical knowledge.

We've had the opportunity to meet a lot of amazing people in general since being in 1D. Meeting Jay-Z was a good moment, and Robbie Williams is always really nice and friendly – we've played *FIFA* with him on a few occasions.

I've always been a big fan of Michael Bublé, so it gave me a kick to hear that he happened to get into the same lift as my mom and dad when we were performing at Madison Square Garden. My dad is so funny – he said to him: "I think you might know my son, he's in One Direction..."! Michael said he loved us and gave his number to my dad. We've kept in touch quite a lot since.

He texted me to tell me he was going to be a dad, and his wife said I'm going to be a sexy uncle. She also said that she wished Niall was the dad! It's so funny, because Michael Bublé was the first person I ever went to see in concert. I was only about 14 and I was about four rows from the stage, so to be speaking to him as a friend now is crazy.

I also text Michael McIntyre a lot – he's such a funny bloke. I have a habit of texting his own jokes to him after I've been watching his DVD, which I really must stop...

We got to meet the Queen at the Royal Variety Performance, and I learned in advance that you call her "Mam" as in "ham" rather than "Ma'am" as in "calm." Not that I said a single word to her. I was so nervous. I just bowed my head. We were the first people in the line-up and I wanted to watch and see how everyone else acted so I could copy them, but no chance. When she was talking to us I was too nervous to speak in case I said anything wrong.

A great thing about traveling is that you get to buy some really cool stuff. Louis and I bought robots in Japan, but when I got back to the UK unfortunately I didn't think about the different voltages, and when I plugged in my robot he blew a fuse, so now he doesn't work. He's basically just a statue. We've also bought six laser tag guns so we can play when we're on the road – the extra one is for Paul, our tour manager, because he always joins in with things like that.

I've lost count of the number of TV shows we've been on now, but one of my favorite ones was *Surprise Surprise*. We had to pretend to be waxworks and then jump out at some girls. They were so shocked!

Now we're getting our own waxworks, which is really exciting. I can't believe that people will be able to go to Madame Tussauds and see us.

Where
WE ARE

1D in Japan.
18 January 2013

I've still got the same friends back home as I did before the band, and that's really important to me. They treat me the same as they always did. My mate Andy from college moved to London around the same time as I did, so he comes over to my house a lot. Often he'll bring his friends with him, and we'll all go out together. We're quite nerdy and have games nights together, as well as movie nights on Wednesdays if I'm at home. It's nice to do something really down to earth and normal.

My friends and family have been amazing about everything, generally. Thankfully, they can separate the real me from the stage me, so when I go back home I'm just "Liam," and they don't treat me any differently. It's not like we all sit down together and watch TV programs I'm on or anything. If I ever happen to see myself on TV, I can never quite get my head around the fact that it's me!

The funny thing is that sometimes, when the guys and I stand in a group, I'll look around and think someone's missing, and then I'll realize that it's me... I'm so used to seeing five of us in photos.

Friends and family often come to gigs and things, and I got to take my parents to the BRIT Awards, which they both loved. It's so nice being able to do things like that.

I GOT **TO TAKE MY PARENTS** TO THE **BRIT AWARDS,** WHICH THEY **BOTH LOVED**

MUSIC & MORE

The other day someone asked me how it felt when our second album went to number one in 37 countries, and that's when it kind of hit me. To think we've broken world records is just... ridiculous. I was saying to Louis just recently that it's so crazy to be the first people *ever* to do something – we were the first British band to go to number one in America with our first two albums, so we've each got a Guinness World Records plaque.

When I used to go to the library as a kid, the *Guinness Book of World Records* was always the book I'd take home with me. And now we're in it! The plaque is up in my toilet! I'm not usually one for putting up awards and pictures of myself, because I think it's a bit weird, but that's such a special one.

My parents have got quite a few awards on display in their house. Usually when you win an award you get handed a dummy one onstage and you get the real one with your name on it later on. We generally get one each to keep, which is always nice.

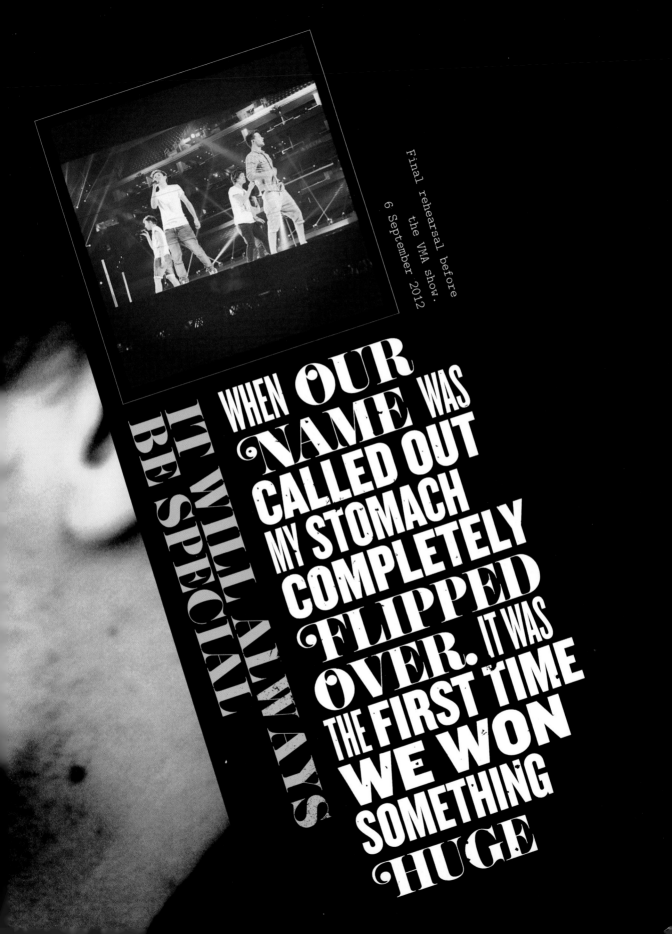

Final rehearsal before
the VMA show.
6 September 2012

WHEN **OUR NAME** WAS CALLED OUT MY STOMACH COMPLETELY FLIPPED OVER. IT WAS THE FIRST TIME WE WON SOMETHING HUGE

IT WILL ALWAYS BE SPECIAL

THAT'S ONE OF MY FAVORITE MEMORIES EVER

ABOVE: Liam and Niall onstage in Dublin. 5 March 2013

I'll never forget the first time we went to the BRITs. I don't really get nervous, but being sat at that table was one of the scariest times I've ever had. I had my back to the stage and I kept turning around to see what was going on, but as soon as they announced the nominees for British Single I was staring straight down at the table thinking, "I hope we win this, I hope we win this." I couldn't look because I knew what a big deal it would be if we won. When our name was called out my stomach completely flipped over. It was the first time we won something huge. It will always be special.

The VMAs were amazing too. When our name was read out as the winner we all bundled on top of each other, and that's one of my favorite memories ever. It will always stay with me. I felt really emotional and it was one of those moments where we felt closer to each other than ever.

People have said that, because we're a boy band, the music doesn't need to be our number-one priority – but for us it really is. It's so important that it's right and that we're involved in every step of the process – that really matters to us. We would never rely on our image and put out an album that we didn't all love and feel proud of.

"Last First Kiss," "One Thing," "She's Not Afraid" and "C'mon, C'mon" are probably my favorite tracks at the moment. They're all quite different, but they all mean a lot to me, and I'm looking forward to writing more tracks in the future.

FABULOUS FANS

Wherever we go the fans are always amazing, and they mean everything to us. Knowing that people love what you're doing, when you're doing your absolute favorite thing, is a brilliant feeling. We still see the same fans now who we saw right back in the beginning, and it's incredible that they've stayed with us the whole way through.

I keep getting told off on Twitter by fans who've asked me to follow them. I'm always happy to do it, but if we get busy and I forget I soon know about it! I have to remind myself to actually sit down and do it. I remember this one girl who was outside the studio for six days. Every day she kept asking me to follow her, then something would distract me and I would forget. I am finally following her now, though. I just need a gentle reminder about things every now and again.

PERFECT
LANDING

EXIT

EXIT

ON THE ROAD

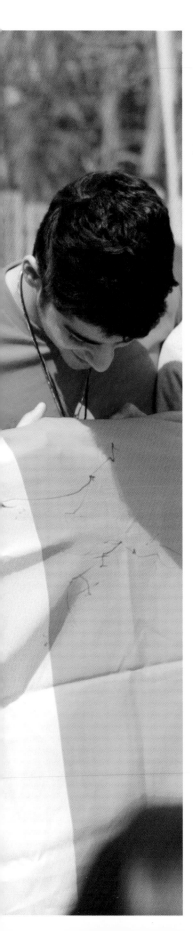

The world tour is one of the most incredible things I've ever done. As soon as I knew we were going out on our own massive tour I felt like we'd achieved something that we'd always dreamed of. It was one of our goals from the word go, so when we were rehearsing and preparing we were all on such a high.

Everything about it is incredible, from the rehearsals to actually being on the road. We did most of our rehearsals in Leeds and we put in long days making sure everything was spot on. I'm the one who always worries that things will go wrong, so I was really on it in rehearsals. I had one moment when I forgot the words onstage, and that made me so nervous that I really pulled myself up and practiced and practiced and practiced. Luckily everything has run pretty smoothly, apart from a few comedy moments here and there.

While we were rehearsing we stayed in a nice hotel that had a spa, so most nights we'd head down there and have a swim and a sauna to chill out. There was no spending late nights at the bar or anything.

When I've been working all day and I go back to the hotel or home, I have to do something just for myself, whether it's going for a swim or playing PlayStation. I like to have that time to wind down before I go to bed, otherwise I feel like I've just worked non-stop.

The tour bus is always a fun place to be. It's great because you have loads of time to phone home and watch films. You can do all of the things that you sometimes feel you don't have time for. I love scary films and action films, and *FIFA* and *Call of Duty* are my two favorite games to play. I've also got a new app on my phone that teaches me a different word every day and how to use it in sentences, so I was using that on the tour bus. The other boys thought it was funny, but I've learned a lot from it.

The only downside to being on the road is that we're often stopping to grab food on the go, so a lot of burgers used to get eaten. But during the *Take Me Home* tour we've all been on health kicks and training, so there's been a lot less of that going on. Our trainer worked with the British Olympic boxing team and he's hardcore, so we all eat really well now.

My tour essentials are definitely my phone, my laptop, the right chargers and plug converters, my PlayStation and sometimes a pillow from my bed, because it makes me feel more at home.

On the bus there's always a lot of tricks and playing around, like food fights and putting ice down each other's backs. But I like to save most of it for the stage. One of my most annoying habits is jokingly trying to trip people up. I nearly got Harry a treat once. I don't know what I'd do if anyone did actually fall over. I'd feel terrible.

We don't have any strict pre-gig rituals, but we do huddle together every night and say some words that mean a lot to us... But generally what we say is a bit rude, inappropriate and funny.

Singing songs is one thing, but when you've actually written something and you hear people in the crowd singing the lyrics it's such a buzz. You can't beat that.

Touring is amazing for so many different reasons, and our world tour is like nothing we've ever done before. We've had a chance to see so many new places. It's like going traveling as a student, but in a posh way, and with shows in between. You eat strange food, you stay in lovely hotels and you have a laugh with your friends. What could be better?

We all see the world tour as our first proper one. I always wanted to do a really big show, and our set is humungous. There is so much going on at each show and we feel like we are proper pop stars, which I know sounds a bit silly.

After seeing people like Jay-Z and Kanye, who had fireworks and these huge sets, we wanted to do something like that too. We've taken eight months off from our lives to do the tour, and then there was the build-up as well, so it had to be amazing. We were involved in every single aspect, from the staging and the set list to the tour program, the merchandise… It's a very "us" tour, and all of our hard work has paid off, because the feedback we get from people is incredible.

Without a doubt one of the best things about being on tour is getting to see the fans. Any time we can stop and have photos taken and sign autographs, we will. Sometimes, if there are loads and loads of people, it's not safe to do it, but we will always do our best. I'm sure there are some very dodgy photos of me out there. Even when you've just got off a 12-hour flight and you're not looking your best, there are always people taking your photo, so there must be a lot where my eyes are literally half-closed and I'm walking around in a bit of a daze.

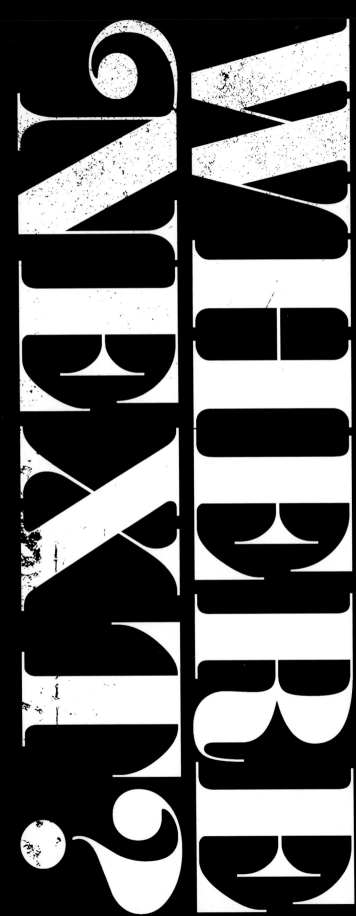

WHERE EXISTS NEXT?

Where
WE'RE
GOING

So what's next for 1D? Well, we're all very excited about the movie. When we watched it for the first time it made everything seem so much more real. It's very weird watching a film about yourself. It's crazy to think how it could potentially change the way people see us because it's so personal. The fans know us to a certain extent, but the film shows everyone the real us. It reveals literally everything.

We never dreamed we would be making a film, but it's definitely one of the things that's meant the most to us. Although after my appearance on *iCarly*, I don't think I'll be going down the road of serious acting any time soon...

Work on our third album is going really well. I love writing and being creative and it's amazing to be involved in making something that people will listen to and enjoy. After we did a session where we were writing "Last First Kiss," I went home and carried on writing, and I was texting the guy who was producing it with us with more and more ideas. I worked really hard on it, so when people say it's their favorite song on the album it's the most rewarding thing in the world. Singing songs is one thing, but when you've actually written something and you hear people in the crowd singing the lyrics it's such a buzz. You can't beat that.

Looking ahead, I just want all of this to carry on. This is everything I've ever wanted to do and I don't ever want it to end. I can't wait to play stadiums. How cool will that be?

WHERE WE'VE COME FROM

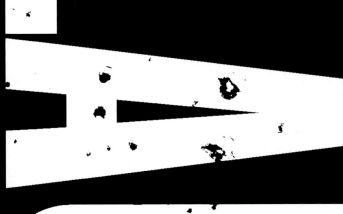

When we first got put together as a group it was a really strange but amazing moment for us all. The week we spent at Harry's house after Boot Camp getting to know each other will always be really special to me.

Releasing our first single, making our first video and going to Radio 1 for the first time will always be incredible memories for me too. So many brilliant things have happened to us over the past few years, but rather than sitting back and trying to make sense of it all, I find that the best thing to do is roll with it and take each day as it comes – I think it would drive me a bit crazy if I thought too long and hard about everything, though occasionally of course it's nice to reflect on all the good times we've had.

Sometimes I lie in bed at night and try to get my head around everything that's gone on. It's hard to believe that it's happening to me. It's frustrating, because I would like to be able to totally step outside of things and look at them from someone else's point of view, but no matter how hard I try I can't. I remember Liam saying to me that things didn't really hit him until he saw the movie. We're unbelievably proud of what we've achieved, and so grateful to the people around us and our fans.

Before I auditioned for *The X Factor* I wasn't sure what I was going to do with my life, and to think that I've ended up being famous and a pop star is crazy. I was thinking about university, but I was unsure whether or not I would get there because I didn't really have the work ethic... Back then all I wanted to do was go out and party all of the time, so I guess in a way auditioning for the show kind of saved me. I never, ever expected all of this to happen, and it sort of took away the pressure of having to make a decision about what I was going to do with my life. I think I would have liked to go to uni for a year or so, but I think three years would have been pushing it!

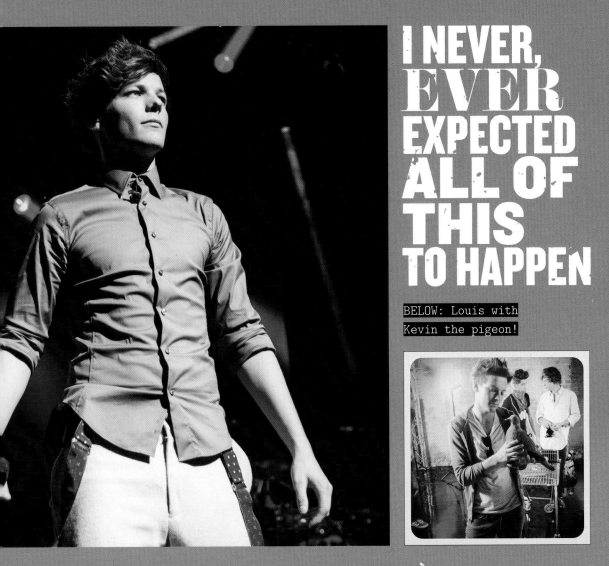

I NEVER, EVER EXPECTED ALL OF THIS TO HAPPEN

I can't imagine my life without One Direction now. We've been to some incredible places and met amazing people.

My main hope for the future is that we all remain best friends throughout everything. I would hate it if anything affected our friendships.

ABOVE: Louis engrossed in a Beatles movie about their first trip to America.

GETTING TO SEE THE WORLD IS ONE OF THE BEST THINGS ABOUT BEING IN THE BAND

I can't imagine my life without One Direction now. We've been to some incredible places and met amazing people. Michelle Obama and her kids came along to one of our shows, which was very cool.

Of all the places we've visited, Australia really stands out for me. It's like the UK, but with amazing weather! The first time we went over there Liam and I learned to surf – that was around the time when things began to go really crazy. We'd been down at the beach surfing for about 15 minutes and then we looked up and there was a helicopter above us.

Getting to see the world is one of the best things about being in the band. Being able to say you've been to all of these places and getting to share the experience with the others is so special. I never want to waste any chances we get to explore, so as soon as we arrive somewhere I'll search out some good things to do. When we have a day off I make sure I never spend it lazing around, because it would be such a waste. I also try to pick up a few words in other languages as well, even if it's just yes, no and hello. I like to think I'm good at French, but I'm not really! I can just about get by, but I would love to learn more. That's one of my goals.

WE'VE DONE SO MANY COOL TV SHOWS AROUND THE WORLD

You learn so much when you're traveling. For instance, I learned that in Japan it's considered offensive to have your tattoos on show, so we wore long sleeves everywhere we went. Liam and I both bought robots in Japan, which was quite random; they're designed to play soccer against each other, and they can walk, clap, do press-ups and pick themselves up if they fall over... Liam's isn't working at the moment, so he needs to get it fixed.

The robot is probably the most extravagant thing I've bought, but the most ridiculous is an interactive mirror. It's in my lounge, but I really should put it in my bedroom, because you can program it to display the weather, the news and Facebook updates. People always comment on it, but I haven't had a chance to set it up yet and I really need to get around to it.

We've done so many cool TV shows around the world. Obviously the VMAs were huge, but for me the best show to perform on is the UK *X Factor*. It's where we came from, so it's almost like we've got a point to prove when we go back. We also see a few old faces in the crew. It feels scary, but also quite comfortable.

Where WE ARE

Despite all of the craziness that's been going on, I can honestly say that we've all managed to stay grounded. It's always been really important to me that I stay close to my friends and family at home. I speak to them on the phone all the time, and they come and see me at shows too.

It would be easy to make a lot of new friends in the industry and get swept away with everything, but when you see your old mates and they treat you the same way they always have done it brings you straight back down to earth. I think if you were to lose touch with the friends you grew up with you'd really notice it. It's the same with the other guys in the band – we would never let each other get big-headed. If anyone got above themselves we would just laugh.

My mom has always really encouraged me in everything I do, so I guess in some ways you could say she's my inspiration for all of this. It was my mom who took me to my first audition, which was for a school production of *Grease*. I want to do all of my family proud, and one of the best things about doing all of this is that I can treat my family and friends and my girlfriend when I want to. That means a lot to me.

It's hard for all of us to get our heads around how big things have got, but it must be even crazier for the people close to us. We live it day by day, but they see it all through the TV and the press, so it must be quite intense. Everyone loves it, though. My family love coming to the gigs, and my mom has collected loads of press cuttings about us – she's even got a full-sized cardboard cut-out of me! She's got access to my emails too, so she can keep up to date with everything I'm doing. It's hilarious.

Louis getting ready
for surfing in LA.
6 September 2012

We're unbeleivably proud of what
we've achieved, and so grateful to the
people around us and our fans.

MUSIC & MORE

From day one we worked really hard to find the One Direction sound, and we did that by getting involved in the songwriting, so it means everything to us that our music has done well. We were all nervous about releasing the albums, and when *Take Me Home* went to number one in 37 countries we were stunned... It's almost a bit daunting, but it makes us feel really proud.

We got a lot of instant fame off the back of *The X Factor*, but it was easy for people who hadn't heard our music to be skeptical about it at first. In a way, we had even more to prove. That's why we had to totally nail both albums and make sure they were full of songs that we believed in and loved. When they were successful it was incredible.

We all love music, so there's no way we could have done a world tour with a load of tracks that we don't like! We're involved with the music every step of the way – and more than ever on the third album.

My favorite song of ours to date is probably "Moments," which Ed Sheeran wrote. I like how my voice sounded on the recording. I also like "Loved You First," and "Back for You," because Liam, Zayn and I all wrote on it. It's about our girlfriends, so it's very personal to us.

Getting awards for our music is great; it feels like the ultimate recognition. The VMAs are massive, so to win there was ridiculous, but I guess the BRITs will always be the most special to us. The first year we went we were only eligible for one award and we really didn't think we were going to win, so when we did, it was the best feeling in the world. Performing this year and winning another award was the icing on the cake. The BRITs have been such a big deal for me since I was a kid. I remember seeing the TV advert for the BRITs 2013 and hearing my voice open it. That was a weird moment.

Louis and Zayn talk to fans online.

hank you, Germany! Thank you, Bambis.
22 November 2012

We're lucky with awards because we usually get given one each. I thought it would look a bit flash if I displayed them around my house, but actually, in the end, I decided that I'm really proud of them, so why not have them on show? I've now got a desk in my hallway and they sit on there, along with my Sellotape and envelopes!

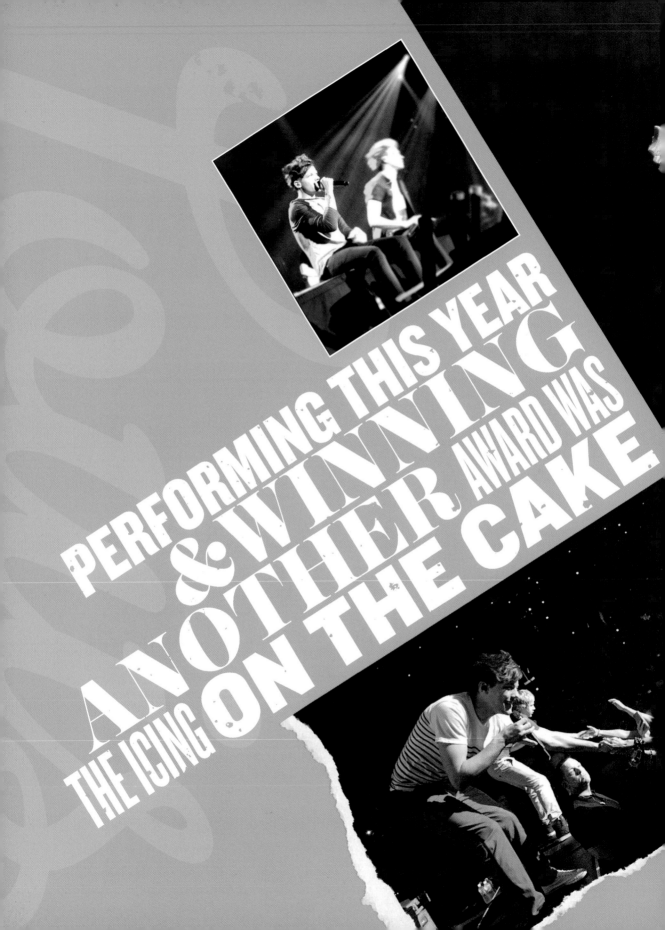

PERFORMING THIS YEAR & WINNING ANOTHER AWARD WAS THE ICING ON THE CAKE

FABULOUS FANS

People often ask how different our fans are around the world, but actually I don't think they're very different at all. Japanese fans are more reserved, but at the same time they're really fun and giddy and they're always *so* excited to see you.

The fans mean everything to us. We've got the most incredible support, and because of that we get to do what we love every day of our lives. There are a lot of fans whose names we know and who we see around all the time. We've got to know loads over the past few years actually, and it's so nice that they've stayed so loyal. We always do our best to stop and chat to the fans and find out something about them. Sometimes, if things are really manic, we'll get moved along by security, but we always try to wave and say hello and sign autographs at the very least.

ONE DIRECTION

OMG!!!!

THE FANS MEAN EVERYTHING TO US

We often get funny presents from fans. Sometimes, because they've read interviews in which we've mentioned things we like, they'll bring them along to give to us. In our early days I said in an interview that I really like carrots, and even now I still get given them. I could have started my own carrot business by now. Most people just want us to follow them on Twitter, though, so we do that a lot, and we try to tweet as much as we can to let everyone know what we're up to.

PERFECT LANDING

ON THE ROAD

We are all so excited to be doing the *Take Me Home* tour – for a start, we love being on the road as it's always such a laugh. And the tour is eight months in total, which is madness.

I always pack at the last minute when we're traveling, so once I've got my bag or case out I tend to grab whatever's nearest. The one thing I always take with me is a hat, in case I'm having a bad hair day. I also like to take my laptop, iPod and PlayStation to keep myself amused.

I find it really easy to relax when I'm traveling, and it's nice to be able to spend proper time with the other lads after the show and talk about it on the bus. That's when we get to spend really long chunks of time together, so we can mess around and vibe off of each other. It's also a great time to phone friends and family, as sometimes you have no choice but to chill out and take time for yourself. I like flying as well, because if you've had a really busy few days ending in a long flight, you can totally switch off there, watch a few films or have a sleep.

We always get up to mischief if we're away from home. We're good at finding ways to amuse ourselves. One time, when we were in France, Liam and I were bored so we snuck out of the dressing room. Our tour manager, Paul, thought we were safe and sound in the room, but we found a fire exit. Then we took a photo of ourselves standing in front of a big group of fans – and texted it to him. He panics enough about us as it is, without us doing anything, so we were in stitches, but for some reason he didn't find it all that funny.

Touring is brilliant. After working so hard on the music it's great to be able to go out and perform it live to people – and no two performances are the same, so you know that every night you step out onstage it's going to be a new experience. It's great getting feedback on our music from the fans too – and we get to see so many on tour.

The *Take Me Home* tour means so much to us, because it's a world tour and absolutely huge. Selling so many tickets was incredible, as we all worked so hard on every single detail.

Preparing for it was a big part of the fun. We have so much involvement in every aspect of One Direction, and we've always got loads of ideas. We got to have a say in everything, and chose the set list for the tour too.

We spent a good few months getting everything prepared for the tour and by the time we went out on the road we were so ready for it. We don't pretend we're the best dancers, but we're enjoying our tour choreography because we're learning new stuff. We love the covers we do – "Teenage Dirtbag" and "One Way or Another (Teenage Kicks)." They're a bit different to our genre and it feels great to experiment.

There's nothing better than coming offstage after a brilliant show when you're buzzing and you know it's gone well. It's especially nice if friends and family are there because you can have a little get-together in the dressing room or go out for a drink. We're not very rock and roll when it comes to our dressing room, though. Other bands totally trash theirs, but we usually end up having food fights...

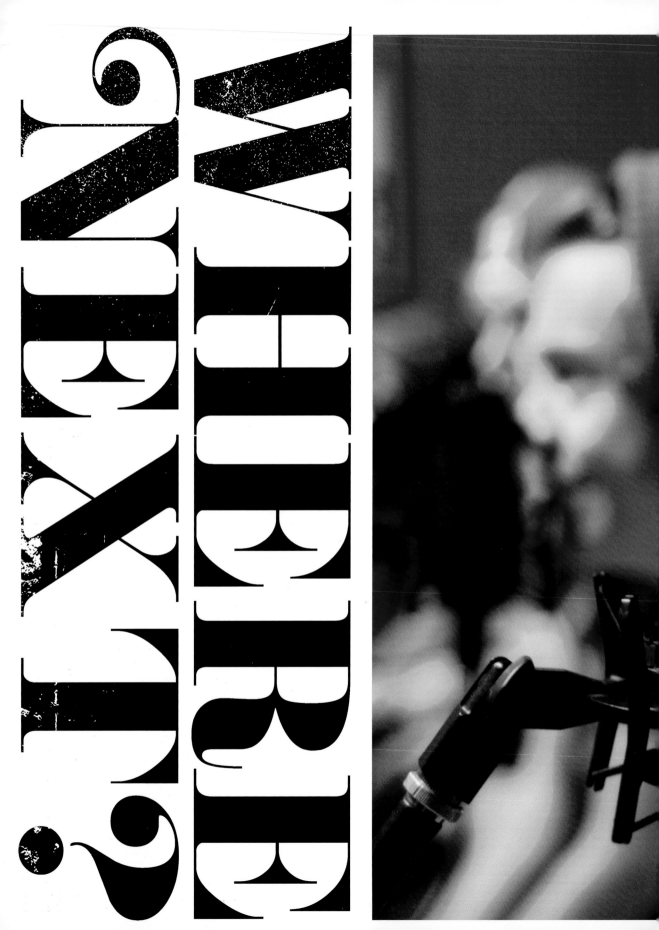

WHERE NEXT?

Where WE'RE GOING

While we've been on tour we've spent loads of time writing new songs. I think with every album we get more and more confident with our sound. I can't believe we're onto our third already. We've had so much time to fill while we've been traveling that I've been constantly writing down ideas and talking to the other lads about them.

I can't believe that we've also managed to make a movie during this time. We all felt emotional just watching the trailer, so when it came to the actual film we were stunned. It was crazy to see how far we'd come.

In the film we wanted to show exactly what it's like being in One Direction, and we wanted to put some of the show in there too, so that people can relive it. It's all the things that people don't usually see. Everyone sees us out and about having a great time, but we do also work really hard, and I think that comes across. We're still totally normal and some of the stuff we do, like playing *FIFA* on the PlayStation, is what millions of other people do when they're sat at home. We're just five lads who happen to be in a band and have a lot of crazy stuff going on around us.

The movie was a real eye-opener for all of us, because it's not something we'd done before. We had cameras following us around when we did *The X Factor*, but this was probably a little bit more intense. I've done some acting before so I have been around cameras at other times, but we all got so comfortable that we'd end up forgetting they were there. We'd do something stupid and only afterwards think, "Oh dear, they've just captured that..."

I don't know if I'll end up doing any more acting in the future, but I've always had a bit of a passion for it, so it's definitely something I'd consider if I got the opportunity. But who knows what will happen? My main hope for the future is that we all remain the best of friends throughout everything. I would hate it if anything affected our friendships.

I really can't see 1D ending any time soon, and none of us wants it to. We're all having the time of our lives, so why would we want to do anything different?

WHERE WE'VE COME FROM

Everything has changed dramatically for all of us since we auditioned for *The X Factor*. Before the show we were all leading very normal lives: we'd wake up, go to school, have a laugh, do homework, play soccer, eat our dinner and go to bed. It was the same every day and I never used to look past the end of the week. Now I could tell you what I'm going to be doing on 13 November 2014. In that respect life now is pretty strange...

I guess the most obvious changes are the fact that we're in a band and it's gotten so big, and that not one of us is from London and yet we all live there now. In fact, I moved from a different country to be there!

My town has around 25,000 people in it and it feels as if everyone knows each other, but I can drive through the streets of London and not know one single person. It's been a pretty dramatic move, but outside of work I still do the same things I always did.

If I get a Saturday off I'll go to soccer, see my mates and have a Nando's meal, or watch Sky Sports all day on the telly with a guitar in my hand. Out of the spotlight nothing's changed, but when we're in it, everything has. I can't really go shopping on my own anymore, so I do most of my shopping online. And if I go to the cinema with the lads we'll go to a late show so it's quiet and no one knows we're there.

WHEN I LOOK AT WHERE WE ARE NOW AS A GROUP IT'S ALMOST UNBELIEVABLE

I've got so many good memories from my time in the band that I could talk for days. 2012 was a crazy year for us. We kicked it off by winning a BRIT award, then we had two number-one albums in America, won VMAs, played at the Olympics and at Madison Square Garden... *So* much.

Performing at Madison Square Garden was one of the best moments of my life. We had a runway built onto the stage that was T-shaped. We came up from the bottom of the stage and I remember looking directly up and seeing the scoreboard with Madison Square Garden written on it and I just nodded to myself. I couldn't believe we were there.

There was a block to the left of the stage that was full of friends and family. They'd flown out to New York to see us, and we all had drinks afterwards, which was amazing: the last time we'd all been together was probably at the *X Factor* final.

When I look at where we are now as a group, it's almost unbelievable. A lot of my mates are at college now, and that could have been me too... Although, having said that, I wasn't great at school and I used to skip lessons a lot, so who knows where I would've ended up? I feel so grateful for everything that's happened, and that's why I'll never moan if I'm tired or I'm missing my bed.

TAKE OFF
WHERE WE'VE BEEN

New York is such a cool place to visit, and I love Australia as well. The people over there have a similar sense of humor to us and they're always up for a laugh. Japan is also incredible – the people there are so friendly and respectful. Plus the food is amazing.

We've loved visiting so many European countries on our *Take Me Home* tour. It's great seeing lots of different cultures, because you learn so much. The contrast between, say, Spain and Italy is incredible: they're such a short flight from each other, but the people are so different.

One of the best things about traveling is trying all the different foods. Italian food tastes so different in Italy to how it does in the UK. It's what Italian food should taste like!

Sometimes we don't get a chance to see much of the countries we go to, which is such a shame. When we went to Madrid for the first time we drove straight from the airport to a hotel – we passed a lot of famous landmarks, but we didn't get a chance to stop. We were in the room for the whole day and flew home again the same night, so we literally only saw the hotel. But on the *Take Me Home* tour we've had a lot more time and get to see tons of places – we take full advantage.

I'm a bit rubbish with shopping when we're traveling. I did buy a soccer shirt on the way back from our Comic Relief trip to Ghana – being there was so incredible; I wanted to have something to remember it by.

Niall

I have honestly never met nicer, friendlier people than I did in Ghana. Making the TV show for Comic Relief was one of the best experiences I've ever had. It was indescribable. About 70,000 people live in a two-mile slum, and it's one of the saddest things you'll ever see, but it's really good to know that people are trying to help them and make a difference. Being a part of that meant the world to us.

Since the day we started out on *The X Factor* we've met a ridiculous number of people. Simon Cowell is still one of the most exciting people I've gotten to know, even though he's so normal when you talk to him. He's just like anyone else you could meet. He likes the same things he always did – women, cars and music – and he's a nice fella who's always up for a good laugh.

Robbie Williams is also a super-nice guy. When we were at the Royal Variety Performance he came over to our dressing room and played *FIFA* with us, and he invited us over to his house in LA. Michael Bublé is also a really cool guy; he and his wife are so lovely. He wants to do a skit with us on Canadian TV. He sent me a text about it saying: "I think you guys are great. You're talented and funny and I think Canada would love it." We'd love to do a song with him. If we ever got to do that I would jump off London Bridge.

Meeting Michelle Obama and the girls was an amazing experience for me because I'm a big Obama fan. The girls just seemed made to be the president's daughters, and Michelle was so friendly. She even invited us over for dinner some day – I couldn't believe that. I'd love to go!

ABOVE: Niall onstage in Dublin.
5 March 2013

Realizing that people like Katy Perry and Rihanna know who we are is just crazy. We've also been lucky enough to do some incredible TV shows. I think the second time we appeared on the *Today* show in New York there were about 17,000 people there. The fans stayed outside in the cold for about a week. A few days before we were due to appear I walked past the studio with my hood up. It was late at night – I had jet lag and couldn't sleep – and there were already a couple of thousand girls there. I would have been in trouble if they'd spotted me, but it was brilliant to see.

It's always good going back to the UK *X Factor* too, because we get to see the people we used to work with and we love performing there live. Our performances have changed a lot since we started out, and it's nice to be able to show how much we've changed as performers.

We love it when we get a chance to perform live. In America we perform in these things called "sheds." They're like amphitheaters, where about a third of the crowd is covered by the roof and there's a big lawn area at the back. You can get about 26,000 people into them, and they sell all the tickets on the night. Playing a show for that many people is incredible – especially when it's somewhere like Dallas and in 90-degree heat. I'd happily play those venues every day!

WE LOVE PERFORMING LIVE FOR OUR FANS

I would credit friends and family with keeping all of us down to earth. It's all about knowing who you are. If you went into this business not knowing who you are and not feeling good about yourself, you'd be a mess. I guess maybe that's why people change when there's really no need to. The way I see it, why would you want to change to become something you're not? Or someone other people consider to be a diva?

I've heard stories about celebrities being difficult, but then we've met the people the stories are about and they've been great – so I keep an open mind. It can just be that someone's met a celebrity who didn't have the chance to stop and chat to them, so they take an instant dislike to that person, who in reality is very down to earth when you actually meet them – just very busy. We try to stop and speak to our fans at every opportunity we get, but sometimes, if we're rushing for a flight or whatever, that isn't possible. But believe us, we always do our best.

We're still just five normal lads; we're not divas at all. We'd find it ridiculous if someone in the band suddenly started making demands or acting like an idiot. There's no way they'd get away with it.

We all stay in touch with our families as much as possible, and I'll never lose touch with my mates from home. Some of my friends are the same ones I had in primary school, and my mates will come on tour with me or come and stay in London. The guys all have friends on the road and we all know each other's mates, so we're like one big group.

When we first started out, the people who are close to me were so excited – they were talking about it all the time, and were really happy that we were doing so well... But there was a time when it was all anyone could talk about. When I went home I told them all in no uncertain terms that I just wanted them to treat me the same way they always had. Once I said to a couple of my mates, "I fancy going out, so as soon as you've finished talking about One Direction, let's go." I was half-joking, but I wanted to know about their lives and not just talk about the band. They know everything there is to know now, and they would much rather have a good laugh with me and talk about soccer than hear about our latest single!

Something I love about having had some success is being able to treat my friends, but I would hate for anyone to think I was trying to show off. I paid off my mom's mortgage and bought her a car – things that I knew she needed – but I don't buy extravagant gifts all the time.

I tried to give some money to my dad, but he wouldn't take it. He'll barely take a Christmas present off of me. I want to do up the house he lives in, but at the same time I don't want to be that idiot who walks in and throws money around.

When I go to the pub with my mates we just buy rounds – the way it should be. I'm not going to be ordering bottles of champagne. It's just not me.

Rehearsing before the iTunes Festival 20 September 2012

IT'S GREAT SEEING LOTS OF DIFFERENT CULTURES BECAUSE YOU LEARN SO MUCH

MUSIC & MORE

We released our second album, *Take Me Home*, in loads of different countries within the space of a few days, and as they rolled on we kept getting told that it had gone to number one in another country, and another, and another. Within about four days it was number one in 37 countries and we couldn't believe it. It was the second-biggest-selling album in America in 2012, and that's just unreal.

Our music means everything to us. While we're happy to say that we can't dance, we know we *can* write songs and we *can* sing, and it's so important to us that people like what we do.

I think my favorite songs so far are the ones we've written and collaborated on. "Back for You" was all about the lads leaving their girlfriends behind when they go on tour. It was letting them know that they're coming back for them. Louis, Liam and Zayn wrote on "Last First Kiss" and I think it's the best song on the second album. It's honest and clean.

Everyone loves the fun, cheesy songs, and I love them too. "Heart Attack" is great to sing along to and great to perform. We believe in our music and I think that comes across when we're performing. If you didn't like what you were singing it would be so boring to have to go through the motions onstage and it would be a rubbish show. That's why we're so particular.

We've loved going to the BRITs the last two years. It's such a buzz, you get such nice food and you sit with some of the biggest stars in the world. Ed Sheeran told me that in 2012 he was sitting in between Rihanna and Bruno Mars, and he said he was thinking, "I'm just this little ginger bloke; what am I doing here?" I was the same. I couldn't believe I was in the same room as such big stars.

Performing at the 2013 BRITs was ridiculously good, and it was the same at the VMAs. Some of the most amazing artists ever, like Eminem and Usher, have played at the VMAs. The minute our car pulled up to the red carpet it really hit me how much of a massive deal it is. We were sitting alongside Pink, Ne-Yo, Drake, Lil Wayne – you name them, they were there. Then we ended up with three awards. Every time our name was called out we didn't know what to do... We were like kids!

I COULDN'T BELIEV
I WAS IN THE SAME ROO
AS SUCH
BIG STARS

Yes, Niall, you are allowed in!

FABULOUS FANS

Every single bit of our success is down to our fans. They've all been spreading the word since day one. Twitter and Facebook helped to get our name out there, but without the fans telling people about us it would never have happened so quickly.

Our fans are brilliant everywhere. We also notice that, wherever we go, they all dress quite similarly, they're all amazingly supportive... and they're all very, very loud.

The power of the One Direction fans is just incredible. The fact that our world tour has sold out is amazing. And we've had two number-one albums in America so far – that's crazy. I've got a shelf in the corner of the sitting room in my house that's full of awards and when I look at it I really have to pinch myself. I need another shelf put up to house them all, and that's not something I ever expected. When we get plaques saying how many records we've sold around the world, it astounds me. It's all down to our fans – that's why they are unbelievable.

Simon Cowell says we've got the most powerful fans in the world, which we agree with – we still see the same faces now that we did outside when we were filming *The X Factor*.

We get given a lot of food by fans when we're traveling, which I love. For example, if we're in Australia we get a lot of Tim Tam biscuits and tubs of Vegemite. I probably get more than the others – the fans know I like my food! They also make the most amazing books, which are full of pictures and quotes; some of them are about 200 pages long! The work that goes into them is ridiculous.

Niall concentrating before showtime in Antwerp.
1 May 2013

On tour you don't have to worry about anything except doing a great show each night. There's a real family vibe and everyone's having a laugh. We hang out after the show and it's a good craic.

The set for the tour is unbelievable – we all love it. The crew were saying that they'd never seen a stage that was so complex before. Our stage manager had been working on the tour set for months and months before we got to see it. We all helped with ideas, though, and when we saw it for the first time we were totally blown away.

One of the great things about being on tour is the downtime. Harry was saying the other day that he had been struggling to find time to practice guitar, but he's getting to do loads on the road. Whenever we're traveling you'll see me with a guitar in my hand when I get a spare minute – no matter whose it is, I'll pick it up. And of course eating passes the time!

We watch a lot of box sets on the tour bus – things like *Only Fools and Horses* – and gangster movies like *Goodfellas* and *Scarface*. We usually get through tons of DVDs and listen to loads of music. I always take my laptop with me so I can Skype people. I got my dad an iPad so we can Skype each other now. It was the one gift he was happy to accept! With my guitar and my laptop I can survive okay for a pretty long time – although I take loads of socks and boxers too!

Traveling is actually one of the most fun aspects of touring. After a show you're buzzing for about half an hour, and it's pretty hard to come offstage after performing to 20,000 people and go straight to bed – in fact, it's almost impossible – so we'll chill out on the tour bus together and spend some time on PlayStation. If we're in a hotel we'll go to the gym.

We get on so well with our security team. They're always up for a craic and we've all got each other's backs. We play pranks on each other and there's always something going on. Zayn and I both do a lot of sleeping, though, so we sometimes miss things.

The lie-ins are probably one of the things I love most about touring. Harry gets up at seven to go to the gym, and Louis and Liam are up pretty early too; I am doing some working out but I'm trying to put *on* weight, not lose it, so I'm drinking a lot of protein shakes to keep my strength up.

We don't have to be down at the arena until about four in the afternoon and everyone is pretty relaxed. We don't need loads of security around us either, so we have a craic with our band – generally it's more laid-back than promotional trips.

If we're doing promo, no two days are the same and things can be quite crazy. But on the road we have a proper routine, which is nice to get into for a few months. Or in the case of the world tour, eight months!

If we're due onstage at about half past eight I'll get myself dressed at about eight and then brush my teeth. Lou, our stylist, usually does our hair just before we go on, and then I spray on some aftershave (even though no one can actually smell me from the audience).

The five of us usually get in a group and say some stupid words to each other right before we go onstage. We have certain things we always say, but in different accents, and we mix it up all the time. We actually get less nervous when it's one of our own shows than we do if we're doing a live TV show, where the whole world can see. We do still get a bit anxious – especially when we're waiting to go on, because we're so excited about getting up there – but if we do something wrong we can laugh it off and everyone will laugh along with us. It's a bit different with live TV.

Doing the world tour is the craziest experience I've ever had. It is the first time we've done arenas, and we're getting to perform in them across the globe. We love both of our albums, so to be able to showcase songs we haven't performed in public before is brilliant. We have a lot to remember when it comes to our set and we have lots of surprises – we're so proud of the ideas we came up with.

We all had ideas and we had a say in every single little thing. Not in a bossy way, we just wanted it to have come from us as much as possible. Things like T-shirts – we didn't just want them to be run-of-the-mill tour T-shirts, we wanted them to be cool and different. Louis, for example, always imagines what kind of T-shirt his little sisters would want to wear.

I play guitar on five songs on the tour and I love that. It makes it even more exciting for me. It's also exciting that our shows are never that structured, so every night is different in terms of how we move around and what we say to the crowd. It's great getting to mix things up a bit.

WHERE NEXT?

Where WE'RE GOING

The third album is coming together really well. The most important thing is that we make music the fans will love. It's probably a bit more of a "grown-up" sound this time around. It's a bit more "bandy" than "poppy" and says more about what's going on in our lives now. We've all been writing loads, and we're working so hard to make sure it's incredible.

The movie came as such a shock when we were asked to do it, but we were over the moon. Seeing ourselves in 3D is crazy, and it was great to make. We started our career with cameras all around us, so we didn't have to worry much – we're so used to them. When we were on *The X Factor* we went to bed and woke up with cameras on us, so we knew what to expect.

We're always doing stupid stuff and a lot of that got captured in the movie. One time, at a photoshoot, I wrapped a bandage around Liam's head and stuck a banana in his mouth and everyone was laughing their heads off, and we were a bit gutted that the cameras weren't there – but we didn't want to set anything up *just* for the cameras. We wanted it all to be real.

There was so much other good stuff that was filmed – they got hours and hours of footage. It was interesting to edit because there were things that the camera crew captured that we didn't even realize they'd seen – we'd be chatting and they'd be in the corner of the room zooming away...

The movie is a proper, full-on insight into who we are. Fans see us on the red carpet at an event, but they don't get to see us getting ready before we go on. In the movie they get to see all of that.

We feel like the movie has kind of documented everything that's happened to us so far, and now it's time for a new chapter. There's so much to look forward to. We're having the best time ever. Fingers crossed it lasts forever!

WHERE
WE'VE
COME
FROM

It's been a crazy
three-year experience
and i honestly wonder
how we got here sometimes.

When I look back at how much my life has changed since One Direction began, I do a double take. For a start, I'm a little bit busier! I don't spend anywhere near as much time at home, because I'm always on the road with the boys. My life has changed so much. The best way to put it into perspective is to say that before 1D I didn't even own a passport, but now I'm traveling all over the world. It's been crazy – we didn't know what to expect or what would happen after we signed our record deal, but I wouldn't change a thing.

My memories of when the band first got put together are great. It was such a good time, because it was all totally new to us, so it was really exciting. I think the first time we ever felt like a proper band performance-wise was on the *X Factor* tour, because we got to do more than one song and put on a proper show. That made it all seem real; everything we'd been working for on *The X Factor* came together. For the first time we could really see where we could take the band.

BEFORE ID I DIDN'T EVEN OWN A PASSPORT, BUT NOW I'M TRAVELING ALL OVER THE WORLD

TAKE OFF

WHERE WE'VE BEEN

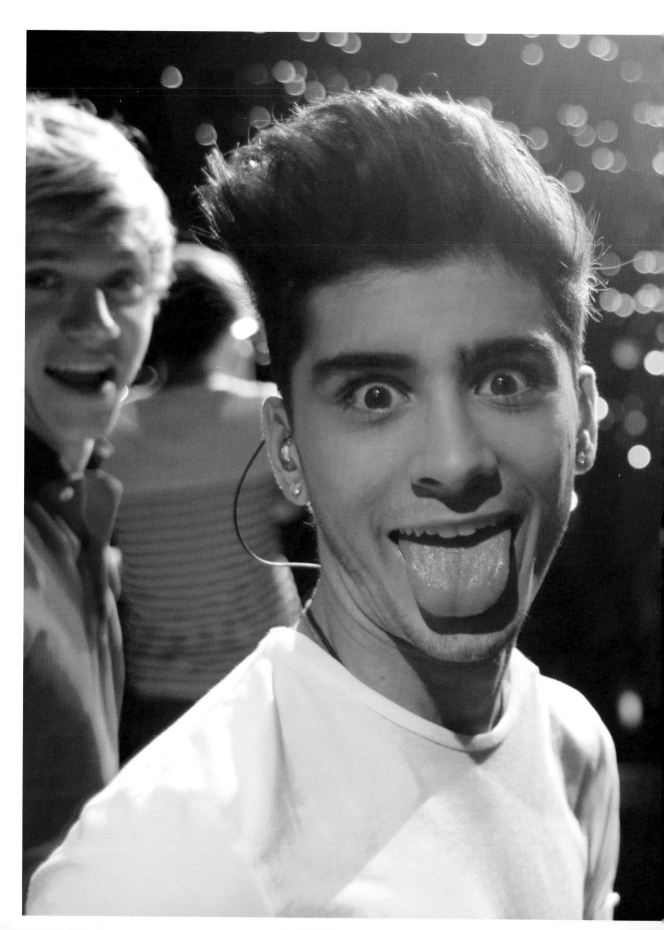

Of all the places we've visited, LA is my favorite. California is great generally, because the people there are so chilled out and there's always great weather; everyone seems to be in a good mood all the time.

Going to loads of different countries is so cool. It's crazy to think that sometimes we'll wake up in London, fly to Italy just for the day, come back home and sleep in our own beds that same night. It feels like a whirlwind – but a great one. People are always so welcoming in all of the European countries – everywhere, in fact – and we feel so lucky that we get to visit such amazing places.

We don't always get to see a lot of the country we're in if we've got a busy schedule – but on the world tour we've made sure we do some sightseeing, and we've looked around some amazing places. We also get to experience new foods, which again is something totally new for me: I'd never tried Italian food before I was in One Direction! Now I'm eating all sorts of things.

We've also pushed the boat out with the TV shows we do. We did a really crazy TV program when we were in Spain once, where we had to do some science experiments, including driving a car over a bed of nails. It was a crazy show and so much fun.

When we go back to the UK *X Factor* it hits me how crazy things have gotten, because it doesn't feel like very long ago that we were there for the first time. We all have a great time on the show; we get to catch up with the people we know who are still working there and it all feels really familiar. We also love meeting the new contestants and chatting to them about their *X Factor* experience, because it's often really similar to ours.

For me, our first gig at Madison Square Garden will go down as one of the best we've ever done, and it's a night I'll never forget. I loved the fact that so many people we know were there. When we stepped out onstage and I looked out at the crowd, I got such a rush – just thinking that it was New York, and there we were, in the city's biggest venue. Afterwards we had a real celebration of how far we'd come. How many people get to say they've performed at MSG? It's wicked.

It's so cool to get to see how other people live around the world, and I try to pick up words in different languages. I'm not that great at it, but Harry is pretty good at learning phrases and things, and Louis's French is impressive too, although he says it's not.

My favorite thing I've bought while traveling is a robot from Japan, but I really love bringing back things for my sisters, like bags and jewelry – I just get them little things I know they'll like. One of the main perks of the job is being able to treat the people you care about and feel good doing it, knowing that you've worked hard for it all.

The most starstruck I've been was when we were introduced to Will Smith at the Nickelodeon Kids' Choice Awards. I was kind of worried that he would be big-headed because he's Will Smith, but he was so cool. I was really humbled by him.

I have so many great memories from live shows and tours, and by the end of the world tour I'll have loads more. It's been a crazy three-year experience and I honestly wonder how we got here sometimes.

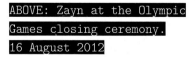

ABOVE: Zayn at the Olympic Games closing ceremony. 16 August 2012

HOW MANY PEOPLE GET TO SAY THEY'VE PERFORMED AT MSG? IT'S WICKED

Where WE ARE

I honestly think the best way to stay down to earth is to keep all your family around you, and all those people who knew you when you were just "Zayn Malik," rather than "Zayn from One Direction." You need to surround yourself with people who will treat you the same way they always did, regardless of the group. I only really had two close friends growing up and I'm still really good mates with them now. Our friendship is the same – they still joke around with me like they've always done. They remind me who I am.

I think people I'm close to find it absolutely crazy that I'm famous. I once asked my older sister if she found it weird and she said that she did, but she doesn't equate the person she sees on TV with the real me. She just sees me at home with the rest of the family doing normal things, like having dinner and watching TV.

The whole thing is weird for us, so I guess it must be weird for our families too, but they all take it in their stride and get on with it. My parents have always been really supportive of me, even when I was just doing little plays in school and stuff – they always turned up to watch me. My mom still loves coming along to our shows now and having a good dance. My sisters love it as well; they come to as many shows as they can.

That Moment when we first walk onstage is indescribable. All the blood rushes to your head, your skin tingles and you feel like you're on fire for about five minutes. The adrenaline is unbelievable.

The most important thing is not to get caught up in your own hype, and it would be easy to do that in a business like this. We have to remember that a few years ago we were five lads who were getting on with our everyday lives, then this crazy opportunity came along and changed that – but it doesn't mean that it has to change *us*.

I always knew I wanted to do something big with my life. At first, that was my inspiration for being in 1D – but that's changed: now it's the fans, the other lads and the fact that I love being in the band so much. Before I auditioned for *The X Factor* I was so nervous and scared, and then when I was put in a band I really felt I'd been thrown in at the deep end, because I'd never done anything like it before. But I've just taken each day as it comes and embraced everything.

MUSIC & MORE

I'm so proud of what we've achieved musically all around the world. We've done things that no other British band has done: getting two number-one albums in America was mind-blowing, and we've had number ones in countries we've never even been to! I don't know how they know about us, but they're going out, buying our records and supporting us, and that means so much. They even buy us gifts for our birthdays and give us cards, which is so cute... Although you do get the odd weird thing sent to you as well. I've been sent a mankini and I also got sent someone's hair once. I wasn't sure what to do with it!

The fans are the reason we are where we are, so they're a massive part of One Direction. They're who we care about. We understand that it's the music that's keeping the fans interested, and they want to be able to listen to something that we have a lot of involvement in. We try to incorporate a lot of our lives into the tracks by songwriting and getting involved in the production side of things. That way we feel more passionately about the songs, and that shines through when we're singing them.

My favorite track from our second album is "Summer Love," because it's quite epic and it reminds me of a movie soundtrack. From the first album I love "More Than This," because I think the lyrics are really clever – when I sing it onstage I really connect with it emotionally.

The awards ceremonies we've been to have been amazing, from the VMAs to the BRITs to the Teen Choice Awards. I guess the VMAs have been my favorite, because all of the biggest stars were together in one place, watching *us* perform.

While we were onstage I looked into the crowd and saw Rihanna and Katy Perry sitting and chatting to each other about what we were doing. It was so crazy! It felt like a dream that I was going to wake up from any minute. The people I'd looked up to for years were there watching *me* perform. Wow!

Each award is like a massive stamp in our career book, and we keep getting more and more stamps. I keep all of my awards in a cupboard in my living room, alongside a load of other stuff I've collected. They literally sit next to random objects I've owned for years and years... But obviously they mean a bit more.

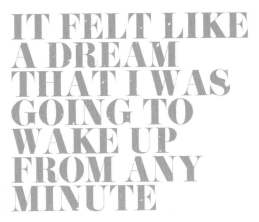

IT FELT LIKE A DREAM THAT I WAS GOING TO WAKE UP FROM ANY MINUTE

YES DUBLIN!
5 March 2013

FABULOUS FANS

Our fans are great. We love performing live any time we get the opportunity, as that's when we get to see a lot of our fans. The American fans are really enthusiastic and they're not at all shy about talking to you, whereas in other countries they can be more reserved. It's funny that different countries have different favorite band members – I've got no idea why that is. For instance, the Americans love Niall because he's got that boy-next-door look. We don't get jealous or anything, though, honestly!

We've been so lucky to have such unbelievable support around the world. The UK fans helped us become well known through Twitter and Facebook, and it was crazy how quickly things kicked off once the word got out.

We know a lot of our fans by name because they've been with us since day one, and we're getting to know more all the time. When we turn up to a show and there are thousands of fans waiting outside, it really is the best feeling. I can't even begin to say what they all mean to me. They've made my dreams come true.

ON THE ROAD

PERFECT LANDING

Zayn onstage at the O2.
23 February 2013

The world tour is undoubtedly one of our biggest and best achievements. We're having such an amazing time and I love getting to chill out on the tour bus in between shows. I've been watching a lot of gangster movies (as per usual), like *Donnie Brasco* and *Scarface*, and I sleep a lot. If you've been missing sleep, it's a great time to catch up.

Also, I've got really into reading again. Some books have a huge impact on me. Plus, when I'm reading more, my songwriting improves – I think my vocabulary gets a little wider, and it makes me feel more creative. I always take my books away with me, as well as my laptop and phone. I'd be totally lost without them. Those things and clothes are all I need.

The other 1D boys and I don't really play that many pranks on each other anymore – we mainly play them on the crew or security, so we'll team up and start a water fight or something stupid. You can go a bit crazy when you've been on the tour bus for hours on end! Sometimes we stay up all night just messing around and talking. (Obviously I make up for it with extra sleep the next day...)

Before the tour we felt a little bit nervous that we were going to see so many different countries so quickly – and be on the road for eight months straight. It's a long time to be away from home. But we're excited because it's giving us the chance to see fans from so many different countries and visit places we've never had a chance to explore. So by the time it kicked off we were all so ready to go. We'd spent such a long time preparing and working really, really hard.

We all decided to get fit for, and on, this tour. We've got a trainer who travels with us. He's intense – my back and chest are usually killing me after a session in the gym – but it makes me feel good, so it's obviously making a difference.

Being on the road is brilliant in so many ways, but what I love above all is that we get to perform for our fans. Being onstage is always fun – it's so loud and crazy – and the *Take Me Home* tour is so massive that we have the scope to do loads of new things: the stage is bigger than ever before, we have more songs to sing and we get to involve the crowd a lot more. It's so important that we put our stamp on everything, because that's what our fans like, so we had a lot of meetings and discussions about every aspect of the show.

I love performing all of the big party numbers that really get the crowd going, and it's brilliant having our own live band. We've got a great support act in 5 Seconds of Summer. We found them on YouTube; they're a bit younger than us and all play instruments – they're a really cool new band. Plus it's good to have another set of lads on tour. We hang around with them a lot backstage and we all hype each other up.

I'm always jumping up and down before a show because I'm really geared up and nervous. I brush my teeth right before I go onstage, for some reason, and we always have a big group huddle just before it starts.

That moment when we first walk onstage is indescribable. All the blood rushes to your head, your skin tingles and you feel like you're on fire for about five minutes. The adrenaline is unbelievable.

On tour we do a lot of flying, so I probably spend more time in the air than I do on the ground, which is crazy considering that three years ago I'd never even been on a plane.

I know how incredibly lucky we are and we dot tale anyting fer granted.

I don't mind flying, but I do feel a bit like you have very little connection with the world, as you can't phone anyone or go on the internet; you just have to watch the same movies over and over again, read or sleep. It can be relaxing, but it gets a bit boring after a while. I want someone to invent a teleporting device which means that you're instantly transported to another country... Honestly, though, I'm not complaining – I know how incredibly lucky we are and we don't take anything for granted.

We're having the most incredible time on the road and it's going to be weird not being on tour anymore when it comes to an end. If I'd been told three years ago that I would be near to completing a world tour I'd never have believed it. I already can't wait for the next one – though we might need a bit of a break first!

When we turn up to a show and there are thousands of fans outside it really is the best feeling. I can't even begin to say what they all mean to me. They've made my dreams come true.

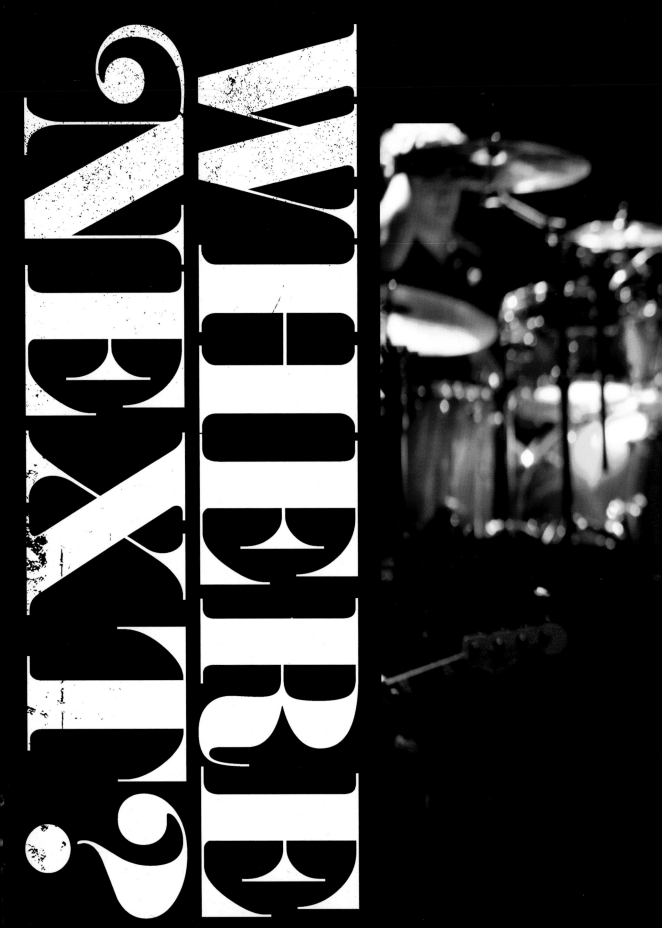

WHERE NEXT.

Where WE'RE GOING

I still can't believe we've made our own movie. How crazy is that? It was really interesting being filmed constantly, on a daily basis. It was what I imagine being in the *Big Brother* house must be like.

The movie is great because it gives our fans the chance to see the in-between bits, when we're not onstage or on TV. It shows what really goes on, and gives a massive insight into us as people. Viewers will get to see behind the scenes; what it's like behind the glamour; how we are emotionally in different situations. They don't usually get to see the real us, no holds barred. I was worried that people would find it boring – and that I'd be asleep a lot of the time – but it's amazing how much was captured. The edit was a very long process!

It's so weird seeing yourself on screen, let alone in 3D. Someday I'd love to do some acting, so I see it as a bit of a step towards that. I don't know if becoming an actor is a realistic dream, but if I got the opportunity and a good role came along, I would love to do it. I'd really like to do something arty and weird, to show that I can act. People would probably expect me to want to do a big-budget gangster movie, but I'd like to try something edgy. I really like British films, so it would be very cool to do something along those lines.

I'm also really excited about the third album, because we're doing more writing than ever before. We're happy that we've been able to take it more in a direction of our own choosing, because we've had the opportunity over the past few years to hone our sound. It won't be crazily different from the first two albums, because we love our sound, but we want to be able to put our own individual stamp on it too.

We have been having the most incredible time as a band since we've been together... and we want to carry on having fun and achieving. I've still got room in my cabinet for a few more awards... Bring it on.

THE GIANT 1D GROUP INTERVIEW

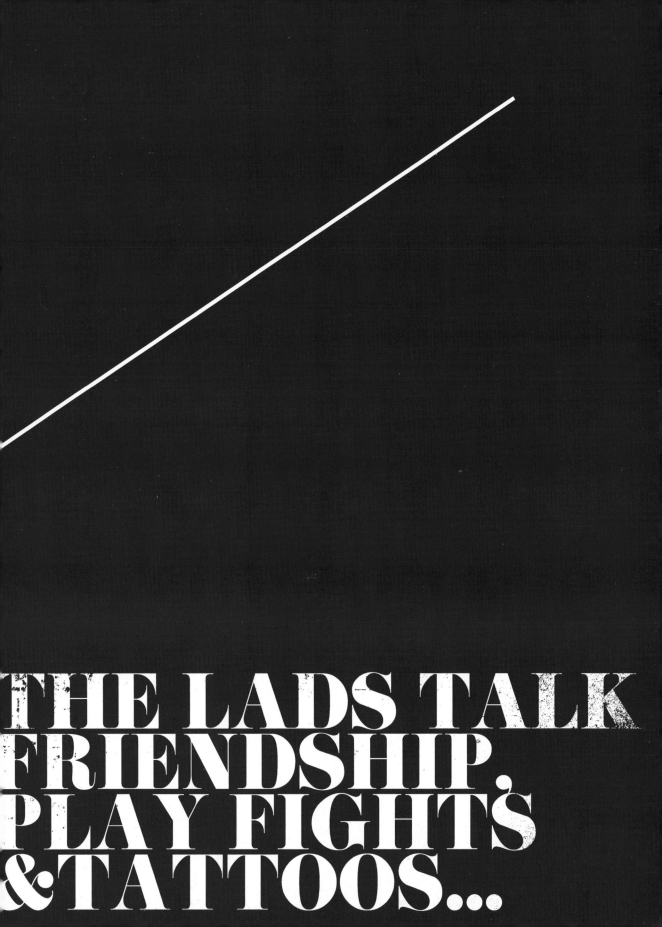

THE LADS TALK FRIENDSHIP, PLAY FIGHTS & TATTOOS...

HOW HAVE YOUR FRIENDSHIPS EVOLVED WITH THE OTHER GUYS SINCE THE BAND STARTED?

Photoshoot while in Japan.
19 January 2013

LIAM: I think our friendships have changed massively, but in a really positive way.

LOUIS: We honestly are best mates. I can't imagine how it would be if we genuinely didn't get on. It would make this job impossible. Even if there was one member of the band I didn't gel with, it would be a nightmare. We're so, so lucky.

Quick cuppa before the show in Glasgow!
26 February 2013

HARRY: We're so much closer now. It's crazy how much we know about each other. We got close pretty quickly and we could be honest and comfortable with each other from the word go, but now it's like that times ten. We know when to make a joke or leave someone alone if they're in a bad mood. We get each other. We know everything about each other's families, and we feel like one big family ourselves.

On the set of *Alan Carr*!
28 September 2012

LIAM: We've always got on, but in the past we used to want a bit of time away; we don't now. We bicker every now and again when we're tired, but we get over it in a minute. We'll go and kick a ball around and it's all forgotten.

The boys being interviewed on *Daybreak*.
5 October 2012

Food on the run.
31 October 2012

1D in Germany.
22 November 2012

Hello, Dublin!
6 March 2013

LEFT: Muchas gracias, Espana!!!
31 October 2012

NIALL: I agree that our friendships are stronger now than they've ever been. I think it's because we're getting a little bit older and we can still be immature and silly, but we're mature when we need to be. There are no cliques or anything; we all hang out together.

SO YOU ALL STILL HANG OUT TOGETHER A LOT OUTSIDE OF WORK?

LIAM: All the time. We'll be at work all the time and Louis will say to me, "What are you doing tonight?" and we'll do some crazy things. We've had a couple of times when we've done all-night writing sessions. We flew to Sweden for one day to do some songwriting and didn't sleep at all. Harry's always up for hanging out, Niall comes out a lot, and we spend a lot of time at Zayn's house too.

1D in Spain.
31 October 2012

1D in Italy.
1 November 2012

LOUIS: We spend loads of time together. It depends what mood you're in, because we've all got different personalities. We kind of hang out with different people depending on how we're feeling. For instance, if you want a laugh, Liam's always up for a joke, and if you want to relax, Zayn's always chilled out.

Take Me Home Tour in Cardiff.
1 March 2013

NIALL: Yesterday the five of us were sat around chatting and eating together - even though we had a chance to take some time away and go for lunch on our own - and that's because we genuinely like each other's company. It's like being in class at school with your best mates.

1D on The One Show.
16 November 2012

ZAYN: It's crazy, because when we started off Louis and Harry were really close, and then Louis and I were really close, but now we're all like a big group. We've all got friends outside of the band, but we all chill together and we have more of a laugh now than ever. The funny thing is that people assume that we drive each other crazy, but we just don't! It's the total opposite. Maybe it's a guy thing, but as we've got to know each other we've learned what each other's boundaries are and what's going to annoy someone, so you learn not to do it. In the early days any disputes we had were accidental and it was just because we didn't know each other as well as we could have done, but now we'll go out of our way not to wind each other up. We just have a laugh and we support each other. We've all got a really similar sense of humor so it's very easy. It would be crazy if we didn't get on, because a lot of the time we practically live with each other.

Saying hi to the fans.
12 October 2012

HOW DO YOU THINK THE OTHER BAND MEMBERS HAVE CHANGED SINCE 1D STARTED?

Performing at the Olympics closing ceremony is a career highlight.
16 August 2012

Harry onstage in Dublin.
5 March 2013

All these mics need are some pop stars.

LOUIS: I'd like to think we haven't really changed as people. We've probably grown up a bit, because we don't live with our parents and we've got responsibilities now.

NIALL: At the same time we still mess around so much, though. For instance, recently we made up a song about KFC with our full band backing us. We still love to have a laugh. We can be totally serious when it's called for, but we are who we are and we're all pretty chilled out. We all came into the band as genuine people and that hasn't changed.

LIAM: I don't think anyone has changed that much. Louis is more organized now than he used to be. He's on top of his emails and everything and he makes me look bad. Harry's come out of his shell a lot. When we first got together he wasn't as loud as he is now. Niall's settled into himself a bit, and he had to move to London from a different country for the band, which is a big deal. Zayn's the same. Zayn's just Zayn.

Bringing 1D to the US!
9 November 2012

In the studio.
16 August 2012

HARRY: Zayn likes being around us lot, but he also likes time on his own. Liam messes around a lot more than he used to. Niall is just the same, and so is Louis. Louis is still loud and mischievous - he likes to test the boundaries. He's quite outspoken. You need someone like that, because he's great at standing up for us as a band.

ZAYN: From my point of view, Harry's grown up a lot since the band first started; he's more confident and independent now. Louis has stayed exactly the same. He's always been crazy and he still is. Niall has stayed the same, but Liam's loosened up a bit. He was a bit stiff before. Sorry, Liam! I don't think I've changed that much. I'm probably a bit more confident now, but aside from that I've got the same beliefs and morals and I'm the same dude.

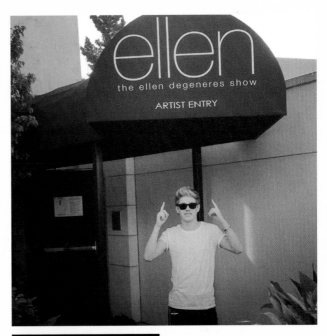

The lads appear on the mighty *Ellen* show.
13 November 2012

The boys rehearsing for the VMAs.
4 September 2012

LIAM: I've changed in that I like going to clubs now. I didn't used to, but I go quite a lot now with different friends. I guess another change for me is my tattoos. When I first got my main arm tattoo done I did wonder if it was a bit big and if I might regret it later on, but at the moment I love it. I'm getting some more done around it too - much to the disappointment of my mother! - so it probably won't look as big then.

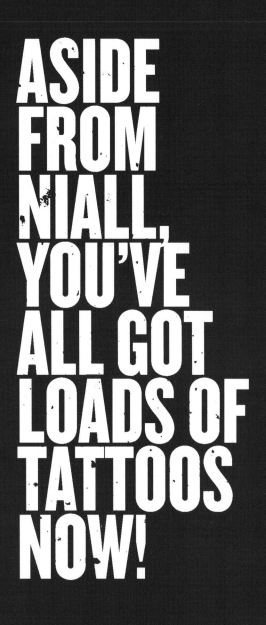

HARRY: I keep thinking up new ones that I want to get, so I reckon I'll get a few more soon.

LIAM: We've all become big tattoo fans, apart from Niall, who is probably the sanest member of the band at the moment. But I think tattoos tell a story, and I'm really happy with mine right now.

NIALL: I'm not getting any tattoos for the moment. I want the 1D logo on my bum, but I don't know if I'll actually get it or not. It's the one I keep saying I'll get if I do decide to get one.

ZAYN: I've lost count of how many tattoos I've got now. I think it's around 38. I've had a lot of my arm filled in now and I still want to get some more.

LOUIS: Once you get one it's like you can't stop. I wouldn't be surprised if I end up with more as well.

Boys during promo in Ireland.
12 October 2012

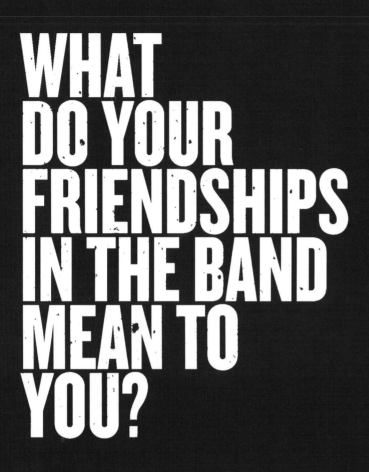

WHAT
DO YOUR
FRIENDSHIPS
IN THE BAND
MEAN TO
YOU?

On the promo circuit.
26 September 2012

LIAM: Loads. I don't think I would have had these kinds of friendships if I hadn't been in the band. I'm still friends with my mates from home, but it's different when you spend as much time together as we do. I know it sounds clichéd, but we are like brothers.

More promo in London.
26 October 2012

NIALL: None of this would have happened if we weren't genuine friends. We wouldn't have had anywhere near the success we've had, because people would be able to spot it if we didn't get along.

LOUIS: Our friendships are really important for our sanity and for the band. A big reason why people like us is that they can see that we're having a good time together.

Soundcheck at iTunes Festival.
20 September 2012

1D being interviewed on the *Capital Breakfast* show.
5 October 2012

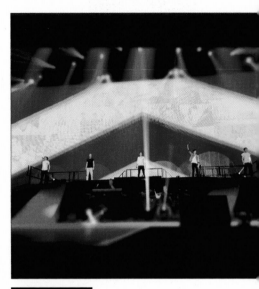

What a show!
1 December 2012

ZAYN: There aren't many people who are in the same situation as me and know what I'm going through, but the other four lads do. We're all in exactly the same situation, so we all get each other and we understand if someone is having a hard time or they want time alone. I know I can trust the boys with anything and they would never do anything to betray that trust. They're in the same boat as me and they're always going to do whatever benefits me. None of us would ever do anything with malicious intent. Whatever is in their interest is also in mine. It's 100 percent guaranteed that we need each other and we're there for one another.

Life is full of difficult decisions…
22 October 2012

HARRY: I've known a lot of my friends from home for ten years, but I feel closer to the boys, having only known them for three years. I was worried that I'd lose touch with all of my mates from school. I don't speak to a few of them as much, just because we're so busy now. But the way I look at it, you tend to make your closest friends for life during your time at university, and these are like my uni years. I can confide in all of the guys and I trust them all completely. That's so important with friendships.

Ciao, Italia.
1 November 2012

The X Factor Sweden.
2 November 2012

OKAY, QUICK QUESTIONS. WHO IS THE LOUDEST?

Liam: Louis.
Niall: Louis.
Zayn: Louis.
Harry: Louis.
Louis: Definitely me. I don't mind saying that.

FUNNIEST?

Liam: Louis.
Niall: Louis.
Zayn: Louis.
Harry: Louis.
Louis: Zayn is pretty funny. He's quietly funny.

CHEEKIEST?

Liam: Louis.
Louis: I reckon Harry.
Zayn: I agree. Harry can be very cheeky when he wants to be.
Niall: Nah, I'll say Louis again.
Harry: I can be pretty cheeky, but I still think it's Louis.

CALMEST?

Liam: I would say I'm quite calm.
Louis: Niall is really laid-back.
Niall: I'm going to say Harry.
Zayn: I'm saying myself. I think I'm pretty calm.
Harry: I reckon me or Zayn are the most chilled out. I've got a pretty morbid voice, so I always sound calm even if I'm not.

WHO GETS AWAY WITH THE MOST?

Liam: Niall. It's the Irish charm.

Louis: I reckon Harry gets away with a lot too. He's got the whole charm thing down to a T.

Harry: I think Louis gets away with a lot because he's good at making jokes out of things.

Niall: I reckon it's you as well, Louis. You get away with murder.

Zayn: I'm going to say me again. I seem to get my own way a lot. Our tour manager, Paul, lets me get away with a lot, and the other boys are always having a go at him for it. If I get up late he doesn't say anything to me, whereas he'd probably tell one of the others off.

Niall: Actually, that's true. I didn't think about that. You get away with a lot where Paul is concerned, Zayn.

WHO IS THE DAD FIGURE OF THE GROUP?

Zayn: It's changed. It used to be Liam, but now I'm not sure…

Liam: I think I still play dad in a certain way. I used to be a bit bossier, but I'm much more laid-back now. I'll only step into the "sorting out" zone if something goes wrong.

Niall: It's definitely Payno. He does still do the dad thing when he needs to.

Louis: It definitely used to be Liam, but I think we've corrupted him. It depends, because on some days some people feel more serious than others, so they'll take the lead. It kind of changes.

Harry: I can be the dad if I need to be and so can Liam, but our tour manager, Paul, is probably the most like our dad overall. He's the sixth member of the band.

Liam: Paul is everyone's road dad.

WHO DO YOU TURN TO IF YOU'RE UPSET?

Zayn: It just depends on who is there. Louis is really good, because as much as he's crazy he does have a really sensible side to him and he makes a lot of sense. He's good to talk to if you want a stable head and a bit of advice.

Liam: I talk to Louis, and also Paul. If anything goes wrong he's amazing to talk to.

Niall: I'll talk to Paul a lot, but I can talk to any of the lads about anything.

Harry: I'll talk to whoever is around, and if the boys aren't around I can chat to the crew if we're on tour, because we're really close to them.

Louis: I feel like I can turn to any of the boys and talk to them. I get a bit grumpy if I'm tired or hungry, so sometimes I just want to sit down and chat with the other guys and get things out. I also find it hard missing home sometimes. The other boys will pick me up if I'm a bit down, and vice versa.

DO YOU EVER HAVE ARM WRESTLES OR PLAY FIGHTS?

Liam: We have done in the past and I'm not very good at arm wrestling. I did win once, when I was going to the gym a lot, and I'm hoping I will again now I'm working out.

Zayn: I've beaten all of the lads at arm wrestles. They don't like to admit it, but it's true!

Louis: We tend to have silly play fights more than anything.

Harry: We used to have huge fights on the tour bus with Paul, but we don't do it as often now because we're worried about getting hurt.

Niall: I once split my thumb open on a watch when I was having a play fight with Paul and I had to get it glued together, so we're more careful now. We can do without more accidents.

The last three years have been unbelievable, we are so incredibly proud of what we have achieved but we know we could not have done it without the support of the team we work with, our friends, our families but most importantly without YOU - the best fans in the world.

We would like to thank Simon, Sonny and everyone at Syco for their continued support. Natalie Jerome, Becky Glass, Georgina Atsiaris, Ben Gardiner, Martin Topping and everyone at HarperCollins for making this book a true reflection of where we are. Richard, Harry, Will, Marco, Kim and everyone at Modest! for your ongoing guidance and encouragement. Special thanks to Jen Kelly, Targa Sahyoun, Luis Pelayo @ L2 Digital, and Ben Gonzalez.

Most importantly, we'd like to thank our amazing fans. You really are the very best in the world. None of this would be possible without you. We cannot thank you enough. We love each and every one of you.

Lots of love,

Harry, Liam, Louis, Niall and Zayn xx

Library of Congress Catalog Card Number: 2013943142

ISBN 978-0-06-221904-6 (hardback) — ISBN 978-0-06-221905-3 (pbk.)

14   15   16   17   18   LP/RRDW   10   9   8   7   6   5   4   3
❖

One Direction assert the moral right to be identified as the authors of this work

With thanks to Jordan Paramor

Design: Ben Gardiner

One Direction's official photographer is Calvin Aurand. Calvin Aurand is a music industry
executive turned live music filmmaker and photographer. For the past 18 months he has toured
with One Direction, using his unique perspective and behind-the-scenes access to document the
band's travels around the globe. For more information visit www.krop.com/calvinaurand.

All photographs © Calvin Aurand, with the following exceptions:

pp. 4-5, 8-9, 12-13, 14, 34-35, 42, 46, 48-49, 50, 56-57, 60-61, 66 (left), 72-73, 79 (right), 81 (right), 84-85
(center), 90-91 (center), 92-93, 94-95, 96-97, 100 (top left, middle left), 101, 108-109, 110, 114-115
(center), 118-119 (center), 120-121, 123, 131 (right), 132 (bottom), 135 (right), 136 (top), 150-151, 154-
155, 160-161 (right), 172-173, 183, 206-207, 208-209, 210-211, 224-225, 230, 232-233 (center), 236, 241
(bottom), 246-247 and 265 © Myrna Suarez / Twin B Photography.

pp. 28-29 (left) and 74-75 (right) © Will Bloomfield

Instagram images on pp. 19, 23, 29, 32, 36, 38, 40, 44, 64, 67, 78, 82, 89, 90, 115, 126, 131, 132, 136, 137,
160, 165, 169, 176, 182, 187, 188, 212, 218, 222, 234, 237, 259, 260, 261, 263, 264, 265, 269, 270, 271, 275,
277, 278 and 279 taken from the official One Direction Instagram feed: instagram.com/onedirection.

While every effort has been made to trace the owners of copyright material reproduced herein
and secure permissions, the publishers would like to apologize for any omissions and will be
pleased to incorporate missing acknowledgments in any future edition of this book.